A CONCISE GUIDE
FOR
OPERATING A RESTAURANT

BY

Lynton Globa Viñas

This book is written in Canadian English.

A Concise Guide for Operating a Restaurant

To:
The staff and owners of *Stacked Diner* in Cape Town, who epitomize what it takes to have a successful restaurant.

And, as always, to:
The man who was once a young restaurateur in Myrtle Beach, South Carolina, learned the business the hard way and who always stands by me with encouragement to reach for the stars –
Wayne Frye

………..*Lynton Globa Viñas*

An Education Research Associates Publication
Catalogue #2018-2453600
ISBN: 978-1-928183-36-5
Distributed by

Fireside Books – Victoria, British Columbia
Part of the Peninsula Publishing Consortium

Lynton Viñas

A Concise Guide for Operating a Restaurant

A Concise Guide for Operating a Restaurant

ABOUT THE AUTHOR

Lynton Viñas has been a general manager and marketing guru for spas and beauty facilities, having worked her way up through the ranks. She has worked in restaurants and hotels. She is an accomplished singer and dancer who has performed at a variety of venues, and has studied at the Cambridge School of Law and at the renowned International Hotel School in Cape Town, South Africa. She is from Cavite, Philippines and loves on Vancouver Island in Canada.

She has worked in the restaurants and kitchens at the Marriot Corporation's African Pride and the Fire and Ice Protea Hotels in Cape Town, South Africa. She has also worked in front office management at the Mandela-Rhodes Hotel Suites in Cape Town. She is the author of many articles on management in the spa, restaurant and hotel industry. Additionally, she is proto-type for the main character in the Lynton demon fighter adolescent book series by Canadian author, J. Wayne Frye.

Her other books include:

Haunted Hotels: Transitory Dances with the Dead
Grand Hotels: Reflections on Timeless Architectural Treasures
Astonishingly Remarkable and Unusual Hotels
Guide to Housekeeping Management

"Restaurants add flavour to life."….Lynton Viñas

A Concise Guide for Operating a Restaurant

Introduction

A Table of Opportunity

Almost everyone dreams of some day owning their own restaurant, bar or coffee shop. Many people do this without having ever worked in one of these places. Unfortunately, the restaurant business is not only time consuming, but actually physically taxing. A restaurateur must be prepared for 50, 60 or even 70 hour work weeks, and one box of steaks can weigh up to 50 kilos (over 100 pounds). This is not a business for those without a very strong work ethic.

A Concise Guide for Operating a Restaurant

The prospect of setting up one's own food business is exciting. But the reality is that the restaurant business is one of the toughest businesses there is. And like all businesses, the key goal is to make money, as unless you are independently wealthy, few people can sustain a losing enterprise just for the fun of being in business. Starting a restaurant is an ambitious undertaking. Many, particularly independent restaurants, fail within a few years of opening because of poor planning. Therefore, this guide is intended to help you avoid pitfalls that can lead to failure. This is not some textbook written by a professor who teachers you how to be successful, but has never actually been in the trenches and faced the realities of the workplace. Rather, this is a book written by someone who has been there and done that!

Effective restaurant management involves several different and distinct challenges. Among them are public relations, inventory control, dealing with staff and customer service. Sometimes a restaurant owner doubles as the manager, but often this is a separate position. Either way, a strong manager is an essential component of a successful restaurant, as he or she is usually the person who handles both the staff and customer issues. There are 10 essential things to keep in mind whether tackling the job yourself or overseeing someone else who is doing it.

Lynton Viñas

A Concise Guide for Operating a Restaurant

The Customer Is Always Right

This is the golden rule of any business. Even if you do not agree with a customer's complaint, how you handle it will determine whether the customer comes back. Truthfully, the customer can be wrong and even obnoxious, but the customer has family and friends, and word-of-mouth advertising can have a good or bad effect on the success of any business, so sometimes swallowing your pride, even when you know the customer is wrong, can add to your bottom line.

Restaurant Job Expectations Should Be Clear to Staff

From the wait-staff to the house kitchen staff, each person needs to be the best at his or her job if your restaurant is going to run smoothly. Proper vetting before hiring and meticulous training are paramount for a successful operation. It is also important to remember that proper treatment of staff is essential to a harmonious operation, and this includes paying people a fair wage with benefits.

Restaurants Need Advertising

Advertising is a big part of restaurant management and it has come a long way from newspaper ads and radio spots. Social networking offers a low-to-no-cost way of promoting a restaurant. As alluded to earlier, word-of-mouth advertising is critical for success, and it can be good or bad, and when it is good it adds substantially to the bottom line.

A Concise Guide for Operating a Restaurant

Watch Cash Flow Closely

Cash flow is the amount of cash coming in versus the amount of cash that is going out, and it should be monitored on a daily, weekly, monthly, quarterly and yearly basis.

If you do not understand this basic concept of restaurant finances, you will put yourself at great financial risk.

There Are Many Different Types of Restaurant Promotions

Promotions can range from a nightly happy hour to two-for-one dinner specials. Settle on one or more that best suit your specific type of customer. Do you normally have singles after a hard work week or is your place more popular for romantic get-togethers by couples or a host of other types?

Catering and Take-out Can Expand Sales

Restaurants have a built-in catering clientele in their customer bases and they already have all the resources: food, equipment and staff. You can probably easily expand into catering large and small events.

In the modern world, the culture of work has often made relaxation a difficult task. The world has, for good or bad, even in socialist nations, become capitalistic in nature where greed is often promoted as an enviable trait. The accumulation of assets is at the centre of all many people do, as a person's worth is far too often judged not by the content of their character, but the content of their bank account.

Lynton Viñas

A Concise Guide for Operating a Restaurant

The work week keeps expanding in many nations, and that can actually be good for the restaurant business, because people are exhausted at the end of the day, and since over 50% of women now work, there is often little time to prepare meals for the family; consequently, calling a restaurant and ordering take-out is becoming more common-place. Also, when delivery is offered, this can add considerable income to restaurants that utilize take-out. In some countries, even McDonald's and Burger King offer delivery.

Track Restaurant Sales

A daily, weekly, monthly and yearly report allows restaurant managers to build a history of the business. It can help analyze sales trends, payroll costs, customer counts and predict future sales. Record keeping can be a tedious task, but it is vital to the success of any business.

Use a POS System

Point-of-sale systems allow restaurant owners to track sales, cash flow and inventory. This simplifies day-to-day restaurant management and helps to trim food costs and payroll, as well as track the popularity of menu items. If you are not tech-savvy, in today's highly competitive restaurant business you are likely to fall behind the competition. Modern technology can allow for instant inventory control, sales tracking and simplify bookkeeping. The high volume of cash and credit cards that pass through a restaurant each day make a POS system a necessity. Not only does a POS system track sales, many POS programs also act as credit card processors. This makes swiping credit cards more secure for both the customer and the business. Servers are accountable for all their sales, and it is impossible to alter checks in the computer unless you have the password. This helps cut down on employee theft.

Update Your Menu Regularly

The price of food can change frequently, so the cost of running your business will change as well. It is important that restaurant menus have prices that keep food costs low and profits high. Also, the menu is often too wide-ranging. If you are selling only a small amount of an item, and it entails excess time and costs in preparation, perhaps it is advisable to eliminate the item. Many restaurants have bland menus when it comes to appearance. Dress the menu up with photos and make sure the type is large enough for people to read easily.

Small Steps Can Save Restaurants Money

Switching to energy-efficient light bulbs and low-flow faucets are just two ways that restaurants can save money, not to mention the environment. Look around your establishment for hotspots you are pouring more money into than is necessary. Also, always be willing to listen to your staff. A good manager realizes others may have good ideas, too.

A Concise Guide for Operating a Restaurant

The Bottom Line

Managing a restaurant involves many different responsibilities, from hiring and firing to tracking sales and basic accounting. There are many tools available to help you manage a restaurant easier, and a good restaurant manager is able to delegate tasks and know when to ask for help. Every step taken should not be just to cut costs, but to elevate the overall effectiveness of the restaurant. A small increase in prices may often be necessary to make sure quality is maintained and that not only do your customers receive value for what they spend, but that your employees also benefit from the effort they spend in making your restaurant a success.

A Final Thought

So, saddle up and let's ride into action. I promise to lay the truth out like a banquet on a huge table of opportunity. However, the table will feature some dishes that may seem less than palpable, but with the right seasoning; they, too, can be very tasty.

The author working in the kitchen with her friend, Thatoo.

A Concise Guide for Operating a Restaurant

Prologue

A Modicum of Success

This guide will help you understand what it takes to succeed in the food business and explain in simple, non-technical terms the first steps that you need to take for success as a restaurateur. There are several questions one must ask when getting ready to open a restaurant.

(1) Are you ready for the challenge?

(2) How much profit should you expect?

(3) Franchise or not?

Lynton Viñas   13

(4) Deciding on a concept

(5) Deciding on a location

(6) Should I buy or lease a location?

(7) Designing the restaurant

(8) Designing the menu

(9) What are the costs involved in setting up a restaurant?

(10) Buying equipment

(11) Raising finances

(12) Forming a company

(13) Registration and licenses

(14) What insurance do I need?

(15) Taxes

(16) What are the best catering industry trade shows?

(17) What industry associations are there for support?

(18) What elements can I effectuate to make my restaurant unique?

No guide can cover every eventuality, but this one will attempt to provide the most practical ways to tackle the primary problems faced and illustrate how they can be methodically approached in a way that will hopefully assure a modicum of success.

A Concise Guide for Operating a Restaurant

Chapter 1

Are You Ready for the Challenge?

In a world where 1% of the population controls 80% of the wealth, the cards are obviously stacked against those of us who come from modest and poor means. We are the ones who do not start our professional careers in mommy's or daddy's companies as vice-presidents. Rather, we must struggle up the ladder of success in a system that is perpetually rewarding those at the top while the rest of us are lucky to get our feet on the first rungs of the ladder of financial stability.

A Concise Guide for Operating a Restaurant

I, myself, came up in intense poverty, going on the streets at 12 years of age with a vegetable cart that I slept under at night, because my parents foolishly brought nine children into a world of want. Through great tenacity and perseverance, I managed to lift myself out of poverty, but as I look at the world I am troubled by a system that seems to always look after those at the top while the majority must struggle day-to-day to simply have shelter and put food on their tables. Still, hope springs eternal in the human breast, and many people manage to go into business and succeed despite the odds being against them. I cannot change the system that tries to make slaves of the 99% so the 1% can live in luxury. All I can do is fight against that system of privilege and try to encourage as many people as possible to not give up on their dreams. If owning or managing a restaurant is your dream, do not let a system that is skewed against you lead to defeat. We must all be willing to seize the day, fight adversity and even if we lose we can stand proud and say we fought the good fight and will live to fight another day. I have been defeated many times, but I always refused to give up, because you are only defeated when you give up.

With the aforementioned knowledge, let us now explore the eighteen elements that are crucial for those who want to be successful in opening and operating a restaurant. This will not guarantee anything, but it gives you great potential for success.

Lynton Viñas

A Concise Guide for Operating a Restaurant

Asking yourself if *you are ready for the challenge* is an important factor. Make sure that this is what you really want. You need to be passionate about your business. If you are not passionate about coffee, do not get into the coffee business. There are many days when you will question why you took this route and you will need to be able to fall back on this passion. Are you prepared to work harder and longer than you ever have before? During your first few years of operation you will invariably find yourself working twelve to sixteen hours per day, six or seven days per week.

Are you good at multi-tasking? As a restaurateur you will have to wear many different hats. It is not just about serving great food; you will need to understand marketing, human resources, finance, bookkeeping and the law.

Also, restaurants have the highest attrition rate of any business. According to statistics, only about 40% of restaurants survive five years. However, franchises (this will be covered later) have a much higher success rate, but require a greater initial investment and the franchisee has many restrictions imposed by the franchisor.

Franchise or not, profit margins are very slim in the restaurant business. A well run restaurant typically makes between 5% and 15% profit; consequently, high volume is a necessity for a high income.

A Concise Guide for Operating a Restaurant

To franchise or not is a crucial consideration when entering the highly competitive restaurant business? Ask yourself if you are better off taking a franchise in an already proven concept or should you develop your own concept? In simple terms, franchising involves paying someone else for the right to their concept. So what are the advantages and disadvantages of franchising?

The Advantages

A restaurant franchise offers you an instant business. You do not have to worry about the name, the décor, the menu or the marketing. It is all done for you.

A restaurant franchise comes with support from the head office. If you have questions or concerns, you can always ask them. This can be very helpful for new restaurant owners who do not always know what to do when they encounter certain problems.

Restaurant franchises have bigger buying power. Food and other inventory can often be purchased far cheaper than through a local independent restaurant. Of course, to this savings you also have to calculate what the franchisor is charging you for using their name, which can be from 3% to as high as 11%. Also, you are generally locked in to buying product from them rather than locally, so inventory control becomes crucial to maintain freshness.

Lynton Viñas

A Concise Guide for Operating a Restaurant

Name recognition is a huge benefit of a restaurant franchise. You do not have to worry about start-up costs for advertising. However, even a franchise must be promoted locally, as people have to know you are there.

The Disadvantages

Money, or lack of it, is often a major drawback of buying a restaurant franchise. Many of the bigger restaurant chains require you to have significant assets before they will consider letting you buy into their company.

There are also lots of rules, as in order to maintain a certain quality of customer service and continuity at each location, franchises have many rules and regulations that must be followed. Everything from the seating plan of the dining room, to the colour of the bathrooms can be subject to specific rules. Make sure you are okay with all the rules beforehand.

Lack of independence is another drawback. Basically you will have to do things their way. You have no say in the menu, the décor or the signage of your restaurant. If you have a certain theme or concept in mind, it may not mesh with a restaurant franchise. You may find yourself resenting the restrictions placed upon you.

Royalties can affect your profit margins. On top of the upfront franchise fee, you are also expected to pay royalties. This covers the advertising, training and other support the restaurant corporation gives you throughout the year. Of course, the franchisor is also making a profit off the initial fee. Franchise royalties are usually between 3% and 11% of gross revenue.

Exit strategy is another consideration, as if and when you decide to sell, the franchisor will have the right to investigate potential new franchisees. So, it is up to them ultimately to decide to whom you can sell.

There is also limited growth potential. Again, the franchisor can decide on whether you will be allowed to open additional units or not. Some franchisors have strict limits on how many units one individual can own. On the other hand, if you develop you own concept, perhaps it could one day be franchised itself. This is where the real money is in the industry. Can you take an idea and not just build one location but perhaps dozens or even more. Essentially, deciding to either buy a restaurant franchise or create an independent restaurant will depend on your wallet, your experience, the time that you can commit and your personality. If you are comfortable working with a team and being told how to do something, a franchise may be the right move for you. However, if you are starting your own restaurant to get away from people telling you what to do, an independent operation is probably a better choice. Admittedly, I am a little biased toward independence, but if you are confident that you have a good idea you could most probably get it up and going for less money than a franchise. Of course, a lot of the guesswork can be taken out of it by looking at the success rate for franchises which are much higher than independent restaurants. However, one must be very leery of some franchise operations. One of the most successful franchises in the world is Tim Horton's, a Canadian dynamo of success that, at one time, was limited strictly to Canada. Started by hockey player, Tim Horton, it went from one small donut stand in 1964 to over 5,000 today and it is still growing rapidly. If you have the money, plenty of it, then this is one of the world's most assured investments. The rate of return is very high for a restaurant (16% to 20%), and so far, not one restaurant has ever failed. Also, one must be prepared to wait a long time for approval, as there is a protracted list of potential franchisees.

*First
Tim Horton's
In
Toronto,
Ontario
Canada*

A Concise Guide for Operating a Restaurant

Typical Tim Horton's Today

One often assumes that McDonald's is simply impossible to compete with. Yet, there have been many concepts that have been successful in competing with McDonald's in the hamburger market. One of the best examples is Wendy's Restaurants. Its founder, Dave Thomas, at 12, had his first job at the Regas Restaurant, a fine dining establishment in downtown Knoxville, Tennessee and then lost it in a dispute with his boss. He vowed never to lose another job. Moving with his adoptive father, by 15, he was working in Fort Wayne, Indiana at the Hobby House Restaurant. When his father prepared to move again, Dave decided to stay in Fort Wayne, dropping out of high school to work full-time at the restaurant. Thomas, who considered ending his schooling the greatest mistake of his life, did not graduate from high school until he was 61 years old in 1993, when he obtained a GED certificate.

A Concise Guide for Operating a Restaurant

Now, here is the real kicker. This hamburger icon actually got his big break with chicken! In the mid-1950's, Kentucky Fried Chicken founder Colonel Harland Sanders came to Fort Wayne to find restaurateurs with established businesses in order to try to sell KFC franchises to them. At first, Thomas, who was the head cook at the Hobby House Restaurant, and the Clauss family that owned it, declined Sanders' offer, but Sanders persisted and the Clauss family franchised their restaurant with KFC and later also owned many other KFC franchises in the Midwest. During this time, Thomas worked with Sanders on many projects to make KFC more profitable and to give it brand recognition. Among other things Thomas suggested to Sanders that were implemented was that KFC reduce the number of items on the menu and focus on a signature dish. Thomas also suggested Sanders make commercials and appear in them himself. Thomas was sent by the Clauss family in the mid-1960s to help turn around four failing KFC stores they owned in Columbus, Ohio. By 1968, Thomas had increased sales in the four fried chicken restaurants so much that he sold his share in them back to Sanders for more than $1.5 million U.S. dollars. This experience would prove invaluable to Thomas when he began Wendy's about a year later. He also had a short, ill-fated venture with a chain called Arthur Treacher's Fish and chips. Failing actually taught him a lot.

A Concise Guide for Operating a Restaurant

Thomas opened his first Wendy's in Columbus, Ohio in 1969. This original restaurant remained operational until 2007, when it was closed due to lagging sales. Thomas named the restaurant after his eight-year-old daughter Melinda Lou, whose nickname was Wendy, stemming from the child's inability to say her own name at a young age. With his natural self-effacing style and his relaxed manner, Thomas quickly became a household name as spokesperson for Wendy's. It is now the sixth most popular restaurant in the USA and is number 3 on the list of most popular burger restaurants and is rapidly closing in on number 2, Burger King.

1) McDonald's ($36.4 billion)

2) Starbucks Coffee ($17.9 billion)

3) Subway ($11.3 billion)

4) Taco Bell ($9.4 billion)

5) Burger King ($9.3 billion)

6) Wendy's ($9.1 billion)

7) Dunkin' Donuts ($8.2 billion)

8) Chick-fil-A ($7.9 billion)

9) Pizza Hut ($5.8 billion)

11) Panera Bread ($4.9 billion)

12) Sonic Drive-In ($4.5 billion)

13) KFC ($4.5 billion)

14) Applebee's Neighborhood Grill & Bar ($4.4 billion)

Lynton Viñas

A Concise Guide for Operating a Restaurant

Today, with over 6000 restaurants, Wendy's has proven that you can compete with McDonald's in the hamburger business. Regional giant, In-N-Out Burger, which is located primarily in California, actually exceeds McDonald's sales in that state. Other chains have also been very successful in the hamburger marketplace as there are over 150 burger chains in the USA and Canada. In Europe, in addition to many of the American chain burger restaurants, there are also over 50 European chains. Another emerging market is China, where in addition to the most popular American brands, there are several local brands. So, when we get to the section in the book on location later, perhaps if you speak fluent Mandarin or Cantonese, China may be very fertile ground.

In-N-Out Burger in Los Angeles Area

A Concise Guide for Operating a Restaurant

Five-Guys
USA

A & W Family Burgers
Canada

Minute
Burger
Philippines

Wimpy Burgers
London

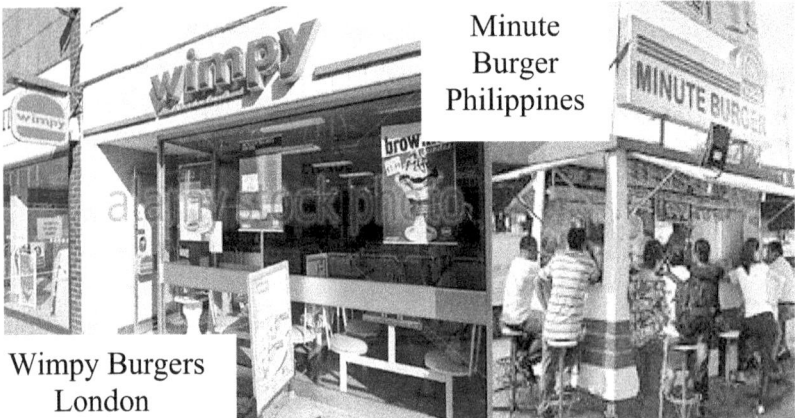

Lynton Viñas

A Concise Guide for Operating a Restaurant

What is my point? Simply put, do not always think it is impossible to compete with the restaurant giants if you have a good idea or even a variation on the ideas of one of the giants. In an economic system where those with power and privilege are protected by the government which responds, not to the desires of the people, but to the desires of the corporations, which frankly buy politicians in almost every country, being able to compete is not only made difficult by your marketplace competitors, but by governments dedicated to serving the interests of those who buy their loyalty.

Still, a tenacious person with access to capital can find a niche that will make success possible. I will not paint a rosy picture, because the road for those of us without immense financial resources is fraught with peril. Still, there are ways for those from humble origins to succeed in the marketplace. Capitalism is probably the cruelest economic system ever invented, but based upon humankind's instinct for greed; it has been and always will be a difficult system to defeat. In its pure form it can actually be beneficial, but today its tenets have been perverted and what we have now is corporate capitalism which is nothing more than a system that allows giant monopolies to erect barriers to make it difficult for newcomers to enter the marketplace. This book will hopefully make it possible for the reader to overcome these barriers.

Chapter 2

Concept and Design

How do you decide on a concept? This entails more than just a mental picture of your grandiose restaurant idea. The first important question is what will be your Unique Sales Positioning Strategy (USPS)? Is there a niche in the market? My number one recommendation here, in most cases, but not all, is to avoid gimmicks and theme restaurants. Restaurant analysts and researchers indicate that most people often only visit theme restaurants once and rarely come back. They have a kind of attitudinal harmonious reaction that says "I have done it once and that is enough." Generally, a restaurant needs steady, reliable customers, not one time thrill seekers. For example, there was once a small hamburger restaurant chain called Casey Jones' Station which had the unique idea that you come in, take a seat and place your order by telephone. There are train tracks about four feet high going to every table and the order is delivered by a scale model train. Now, this was exciting for the kids, but only in a transitory fashion. You do it once or twice and the thrill is over. The chain was an almost instant failure.

Also, be very careful with what you think might be a unique idea, but cannot overcome certain culture norms. There was a man in Arkansas who thought he had come up with an incredible idea. He opened a place called Bunny Burger. Yes, those furry little animals are used as food in many parts of the world. However, ordering a Bunny Burger with ketchup, mustard, lettuce and pickles just did not go over very well with people in the USA who kept thinking about those cute furry little animals and the Easter Bunny. Colossal failure!

There are several steps one can take to analyze market concepts. See what is hot in other markets for inspiration. Or, be the first to market a product or concept, but as alluded to earlier, make sure your concept is workable and will be accepted by the people. Explore these great resources for a little bit of

A Concise Guide for Operating a Restaurant

inspiration: Springwise (https://www.springwise.com) and its network of spotters scan the globe for smart new business ideas, at https://pos.toasttab.com/blog/restaurant-ideas there are a host of great concepts for restaurants. Below are some other great web-sites for ideas:

https://www.thebalance.com/easy-restaurant-ideas-2888618

https://www.webstaurantstore.com/article/149/how-to-choose-a-restaurant-concept.html

https://www.opstart.ca/10-great-small-restaurant-ideas/

http://aaronallen.com/blog/10-unique-restaurant-concepts-in-europe

https://www.qsrmagazine.com/

My husband was once called a marketing genius by *the Los Angeles Times* (a fact he reminds me of often), and he told me that if you want to be successful look at what other restaurants are doing and emulate them. If someone else is doing it right, there is no shame in copying their formula for success. In that respect, look at what the big chain restaurants do, particularly because they spend fortunes on expensive market research. If you are just at the idea stage why not take a grand tour of a successful restaurant? Even get a job in one for awhile so you can absorb some of their expertise. If you are thinking about opening a Southern Fried Chicken Restaurant, take a trip to the southern states of America if you can afford it. Rent a car and drive around, see the best places, eat there and get ideas, collect sample menus and take photos.

The methodologies and approaches to restaurant design are varied. In the United States alone, there are over one million restaurants; each trying hard to differentiate itself from the next. In Europe there are nearly two million restaurants. No exact number is available, but it assumed there are over five million restaurants in China. So, they are numerous and varied. Here, we will explore the design concept for small, medium and large eateries.

Concept Development

Restaurant concept development is more than just the architectural elements and layout. It also takes into consideration things such as market and competitive research, emerging and waning trends, financial modeling, what-could-happen scenarios, branding, supply chains and potentially a variety of other elements too numerous to mention in a concise guide like this. Whether it is a restaurant or other type building renovation or the development of a completely new prototype, restaurant concept development is important because as the saying goes "a picture is worth a thousand words." One cannot look at restaurant design in a vacuum that only involves the interior designers and architects.

A Concise Guide for Operating a Restaurant

Restaurant Design Budgets

In almost every case, the most import question asked is how much will it cost? Obviously, budgets can swing dramatically from project to project, but there are some basic rules which apply no matter what size the project might be and how detailed the concept is.

(1) Generally, restaurants cost about the same or a bit more per square metre/feet than the typical home. I will not attempt to give specific figures, because labour costs vary so widely. However, material costs are pretty consistent. Obviously the quality of the material will have a profound effect on the costs. If you are using Italian marble, it is going to be considerably more than Chinese marble. However, that comes into the equation later when decisions on material to use are made.

(2) The cost for restaurant design and planning is generally estimated to be around 10% of the construction budget (considering strictly the design phases of the project, not the materials used or the larger concept development issues involved in bigger scale projects).

(3) The type of restaurant you are building is certainly a consideration as you spend more per square metre/feet for a fine dining restaurant than a fast-food or casual dining concept. Also, you should expect an entirely different financial model in approaching the creation of a new restaurant concept you plan

Lynton Viñas 33

to implement country-wide as opposed to a single restaurant concept.

When I was a child, my mother and father would often say, "Your eyes are bigger than your stomach." With that in mind, I highly suggest thinking small in the beginning, because the chances are stacked against anyone becoming a McDonald's or Burger King overnight. Twenty-five to thirty years is probably the norm for chains to really take-off. My husband, who was in the restaurant business in Myrtle Beach, South Carolina, once told me, "Never think too big, because if you do you will lose sight of what is right before your eyes. One restaurant operated efficiently which dispenses fine food that generates good word-of-mouth advertising and a nice profit margin may well exceed a dozen restaurants operated poorly because of a lack of proper oversight." Our ideas most times exceed the realities of the real world. It is more than just wishful thinking to believe success can be duplicated without the immense financial resources needed to effectuate growth. As astute as he was, Harlan Sanders was not the real reason KFC grew into a world-wide chicken restaurant powerhouse phenomena. Colonel Sanders, although wealthy, simply did not have the financial resources to make his restaurants a world-wide household name. That was done by a venture capitalist, John Y. Brown. Consequently, most growth is limited; because very few people have access to

A Concise Guide for Operating a Restaurant

the finances necessary to launch a nationwide chain overnight. In fact, there have been some colossal failures over the years, primarily because of under capitalization. Some of the most noted failures include the following:

These two restaurant chains burst forth almost overnight, but under capitalization doomed them almost from the start. Lesson learned: do not expand too quickly.

A Concise Guide for Operating a Restaurant

Of course, even well-capitalized ventures can also fail, not because of a lack of funds, but because of a lack of proper management. The roadside restaurant concept was developed by Howard Johnson in 1929 right before the Great Depression, as he saw the growing car industry and the expanding roadways of the United States as a panacea for the restaurant business. They gave away free postcards, so that people could write home about their travels and provide the restaurant with free advertising in the process. Over the years, this iconic chain slowly faded from the scene as it did not modernize its restaurants or keep up with changing dining trends. After close to 100 years, there is now only one restaurant left and although it goes by the Howard Johnson's name, it has been in private hands for many years.

Sample Howard Johnson's post card 1936

Lynton Viñas

A Concise Guide for Operating a Restaurant

Can a new prototype for a franchise be created for little money? Of course it can and if you have a good idea, lenders might offer funds, but, of course, as always in these situations, it will be the banks that get repaid first.

I am not trying to put a damper on an individual's hopes and dreams, only offering a candid assessment of the way things are. Capitalism has no heart or soul as evidenced by the legions of poor who must toil in obscurity. Its only purpose is to generate wealth, and unfortunately, most of that wealth flows to the top of the economic ladder, and those of us below that top rung get the scraps from the table of plenty set for the wealthy and the corporations. This does not mean we cannot succeed, but it does mean we have to work doubly hard to do so. For the small entrepreneur, the road is long, filled with many curves, hills, bumps and pot holes. One of the greatest assets one must have is perseverance, because the landscape of capitalism is often a desert of lost hope where only those with great stamina will survive. In my own life, I have often faced obstacles that made me want to simply give up, but somewhere deep within I found the strength to go on. For those of us who come from severe poverty, we often feel that we are in a deep abyss where the sunlight of hope rarely can reach us. I understand why so many do give up, because it seems that hope is something that died along with compassion. Yet, there is that small glimmer of hope that can shine through the clouds of despair. Fortified with knowledge and a strong will, giving-up should never be an option.

Restaurant Design Considerations

There are countless elements to take in to consideration in restaurant design. Today's successful restaurant concepts are about more than just great food, great service and great atmosphere. The following list is not completely comprehensive, or in any order of priority, but provides a sense of how complex these projects can be and why it can often be money well spent, if one can afford it, to bring in outside help.

(1) Brand Personality Concept: Brands, just like people, have personalities. A person can become known for acting or behaving a certain way. So too can a brand. The personality of a brand should be defined in intricate detail. This should happen before the first sketch of the restaurant design is even considered. Branding is the core from which all else flows. A brand tells customers what a restaurant is all about. It sets the restaurant apart from its competitors and creates a personality. When done well, a brand gives visual and emotional cues to potential customers. A strong restaurant brand extends across all parts of the business, from the interior design to the marketing materials. Developing a brand and using it as an advantage can give a restaurant owner a competitive edge. A brand is more

than a logo. It encompasses the overall experience of dining at the restaurant. It starts with a core idea that motivates the business, like serving gourmet comfort food or providing a new ethnic food experience. The core idea becomes the public brand promise, which is communicated to customers through marketing and advertising. The visual aspects of a brand support the brand promise through the logo, colours, fonts and image styles. Since restaurant dining is a sensory experience, the brand must involve a range of elements that ultimately affect the customer. A successful restaurant brand is evident in everything a customer interacts with, from advertisements to the way food is presented to the signs over bathroom doors. The visual aspects and style are applied to marketing materials like a website, menu, take-out boxes, advertisements and business cards.

Brand Business Card

Brand Personality Concept

A Concise Guide for Operating a Restaurant

(2) Brand Promises: Most of us like to think that we are examples of rock-solid integrity. However, if you look at the definition, it is easy to see that far too many people actually fall short. Integrity is defined as *the quality of being honest and having strong moral principles and uprightness.* Good synonyms for the term *integrity* are honesty, probity, rectitude, honour, good character, principled, ethical, moral, righteous, virtuous, decent, fair and sincere.

Making a promise that your brand will live up to all of the above is no easy task, and in a world filled with condemners and finger-pointers, it is becoming increasingly difficult to foster a culture that promotes integrity. When it is considered good business for a banker to steal more with a stroke of a pen than a robber can steal with a gun, we have reached a time when integrity in the marketplace is sorely lacking. For a brand to have integrity, one must establish its distinct set of promises that differentiate it and define it from other brands. This is imperative to set your brand apart.

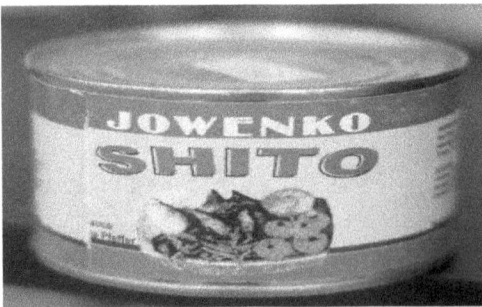

Unusual branding can work, but sometimes going over the top can be a bit much. This does not work for me, but the brand has been around for many years, so perhaps they know something I don't.

A Concise Guide for Operating a Restaurant

(3) Brand Positioning: Being the best at something takes an effort, and it must also be noted that rarely are any of us the best at any particular thing. There is always someone better, if not now, on the horizon. However, striving to be the best means that we are always making a maximum effort. Do not accept mediocrity in your brand whether you have a three seat hotdog stand or an Italian marble columned rooftop restaurant at the Empire Sate Building.

(4) Silverware: Rarely do we think consciously about silverware when eating in a restaurant, but it is a precursor to any meal. For example: light, flimsy, cheap silverware will give an impression of light, flimsy and cheap food. That is why many high-end restaurants use large and heavy utensils. Like the table upon which these items set, the cleanliness and appearance of the silverware on a well-set table add to the dining experience.

A Concise Guide for Operating a Restaurant

(5) Uniforms: Restaurant uniforms have come a long way since the day of the fine dining tuxedo. Even high-end fashion designers are now involved in making uniforms for restaurant workers. Some chains have tens of thousands of employees and each is a symbolic ambassador for the brand. The uniform is an extension of the brand and therefore should be viewed through the same lens as your overall restaurant design process.

Uniforms are just another way to show customers what your restaurant is all about. Whether it is a casual restaurant with silly sayings on the backs of t-shirts or an upscale restaurant where servers wear ties, uniforms help set the tone. If customers need something, how will they flag down an employee if they are all dressed differently? You certainly do not want customers to accidentally ask another diner for a refill! Uniforms make it easy for customers to spot employees at a glance.

When uniforms look great and fit well, they make employees feel proud of their jobs. This is one reason to make sure your uniforms are not embarrassing or ill-fitting. After all, who feels good when they are wearing baggy shirts or goofy-looking hats? If your employees know they look great and professional, they are more likely to feel proud to work at your restaurant. Of course there are exceptions to the rule, as some themed restaurants might actually have crazy-looking uniforms as part of the branding. Also, places like *Hooters* have distinctive uniforms for an obvious reason, and are made with a certain type of clientele in mind.

Employees have very different backgrounds and lifestyles, but when they put their uniforms on they are all part of the same team. Uniforms can help create a professional environment and can assist employees with getting in the right frame of mind to do a great job.

The food and service might be great, but for many customers, the appearance of servers makes a big difference. Simply put, uniforms make employees look reliable and trustworthy. This lets customers know that they can count on them to do their jobs right.

It is important that overall appearance project a clean image. Some of the most basic compliments to clean, stylish uniforms are obvious: hair that is styled or held back so that it does not get into customers' food, neat and trimmed nails and no dangling jewellery. Despite their general acceptance, tattoos and piercings have an unclean image, so, in most cases, they should be covered. This is important because it influences the perception of the food and the quality of service. Customers feel better about being served by people who are visibly clean.

Although uniforms look different at each restaurant, there is no denying that appearances are important. The right uniforms and the right grooming can define a brand, mark employees as clean, inspire employee pride, create a professional environment and inspire customer confidence.

A Concise Guide for Operating a Restaurant

(6)Ventilation: I realize this is seemingly an area that is not considered as important as others, but this is actually one of the most critical elements in concept and design. Many places around the world have made it illegal to smoke in restaurants, and now in some more advanced countries, even in public places. It appears that the tobacco death dealers have finally been somewhat corralled as a result of public pressure that has moved politicians to act for the public good rather than the corporate good. Despite this new attitude, ventilation is still important for keeping the air clean.

When air is taken from the kitchen it must be replaced by clean, fresh air in order for the kitchen to not become noxious, and these odours can also filter into the dining area. This is where make-up air becomes important. Make-up air is outside air that is brought into a restaurant through the ventilation system. Having a source of make-up air that delivers clean outdoor air consistently is the best way to ensure proper ventilation is providing the restaurant with the best possible results in air quality. An establishment that does not have enough make-up air being delivered will develop negative pressure. Having negative pressure in a restaurant can significantly lower the performance of the kitchen exhaust system and cause uncomfortable conditions for both employees and customers.

A Concise Guide for Operating a Restaurant

Some signs of an establishment not having enough make-up air provided are as follows:

- The building has temperature changes that can be felt when moving from one area to another.

- Doors leading to the exterior will slam shut when left open.

- Ventilation systems do not perform at as high a level as expected.

- Cold air can be felt coming in through any cracks or other openings.

Making sure a restaurant has an adequate supply of make-up air is an integral part in creating an environment everyone can enjoy; consequently, making sure there is a proper ventilation system should be part of any concept design.

(5) Bathrooms & Brand Immersion: It may seem trivial, but making sure the bathroom is always spotlessly clean and well-presented is reflective in the customers' minds of the overall cleanliness of the restaurant. In other words, an unkempt bathroom must mean an unkempt kitchen. "If they allow their bathrooms, which are in plain sight of customers, to be disgustingly untidy, what must the kitchen look like since it is out of view?" At the concept design stage it should be apparent that the bathroom presents an opportunity to further differentiate a restaurant and make an impression. You should

be able to put a blindfold on a customer, drive them across the city, put them in your bathroom and take off the blindfold and they should be able to tell you exactly where they are. That is great bathroom design which is distinctive and communicative of the brand. So, is this design or is this marketing? The two are actually inextricably intertwined.

A bathroom can actually part of the dining experience.

(4) Door Knobs and Doors Can Speak: The expression "dumb as a doorknob" can be relevant to a restaurant. Doorknobs can actually communicate a lot about a restaurant by speaking before the hostess or greeter welcomes the customer.

A Concise Guide for Operating a Restaurant

The texture, the weight, the materials, the style and nature of the doorknob all communicate the brand. The doorknob is the first thing customers lay their hands on. The old saying 'initial impressions count' is vital here. Are the door handles going to create the initial impression that you want? Are they going to give the feeling that the customer is entering into what will lend pleasure for the eyes and the palate?

The doors themselves are also a way for branding. The casual dining restaurant will have different doors than the upscale, fine dining restaurant. Never underestimate the lure of a nice door and a nice door handle.

(5) Restaurant Menu Design: The most important piece of marketing collateral for a restaurant is its menu. A menu can not be viewed as simply an inventory of items for sale with a corresponding price. It must be viewed as the single most important tool in showcasing a restaurant's offerings, culinary philosophy and brand attributes. The weight, size, paper-type, presentation, fonts, photos and use of language are all important considerations. The menu should be viewed as an extension of

the restaurant design, fully integrated in the brand personality and positioning. A restaurant might have the best food in town, but that does not preclude the need for an effective menu.

A few simple steps to plan, organize and design the menu can make a world of difference to a restaurant's success. Here are 19 ideas that can help a restaurant owner in elevating a menu to more than just a list of items for sale.

ORGANIZE YOUR MENU LOGICALLY

Do not make your customers perform a scavenger hunt when they just want to eat. Make it easy for them to find what they want by organizing in a way that makes sense - appetizers first, desserts last, etc.

GIVE YOUR BEST DISHES THE BEST PLACEMENT

This might seem obvious, but do not hide star items. Put them front and center where they are easy to find. Customers' eyes are most often drawn to the upper right hand corner or the center of the page, so consider placing the biggest sellers in these locations.

BE RESOURCEFUL

Do you have a burger on your menu? Add a few different toppings or a new sauce and you have an entirely different menu item without adding much cost. And if you offer a shrimp salad, create a shrimp pasta, pizza or risotto dish as well to get the most out of your ingredients.

A Concise Guide for Operating a Restaurant

CREATE SOMETHING SPECIAL

Many menus feature pizza, sandwiches, or salads, so make yours stand out. Try tweaking a classic by adding a signature change that fits your restaurant's brand.

KEEP YOUR LANGUAGE SIMPLE

You might think your double entendres are funny and your pretentious cooking terms are sophisticated, but they will probably just annoy customers. It is okay to show some personality, but keep the focus on your food, not words. (A mouth-watering picture is worth a thousand words.)

KEEP IT MANAGEABLE

Simply put, one restaurant can not possibly excel at every dish on a ten page menu. It is better to keep your menu on the shorter side and spotlight your strong points. Customers would rather choose from 10 amazing dishes than 100 ordinary ones.

UPDATE WHEN YOU NEED TO

Food prices and availability change, so should your menu. Feel free to remove something that has become too costly or to add in a few seasonal items.

CHOOSE THE RIGHT VISUALS

Do not decorate your menu with generic clip-art; this is distracting and does not add much for your customers. On the other hand, if you decide to include photos of your actual food, be sure to choose photos that make your dishes look as

Lynton Viñas

appetizing as possible. Food photography is tricky, so you might want to consider hiring a professional photographer.

PROOFREAD

What is more unappetizing than a typo? You definitely do not want your customers to notice your mistakes instead of your food. Do not just rely on spell-check; be sure to have many people look for errors.

KEEP IT SHORT

Remember, you are writing a menu, not a novel. Of course you want to include relevant information that will make your dishes sound delicious, but make sure your descriptions do not get too long.

PAY ATTENTION TO COLOUR

What kind of cuisine do you serve? Does your restaurant have a theme? The answers to these questions can influence the colours you choose for your menu.

WATCH YOUR FONTS

Never use a font that is hard to read. If your customers can not read your menu, they become frustrated.

DO NOT LAMINATE

Once your menu is laminated, you are stuck with. You will probably want to change your menu at least once a year, so use plastic covers that make it easy to slide in a new menu. Also, some restaurants with limited offerings use placemats as menus.

A Concise Guide for Operating a Restaurant

. GET FEEDBACK

Have some customers read over your menu and give you their honest opinions. Does everything look good? Are your descriptions confusing? What needs to change?

KNOW YOUR COMPETITION

Know what your competitions' menus are like. How can you make your menu stand out from theirs?

USE NUMBERS IF YOU NEED THEM

Does your restaurant serve a cuisine that is not necessarily familiar to customers? Customers might be reluctant to order something they can not pronounce, so consider numbering meals to make it easier on them.

HAVE MORE THAN ONE MENU

Remember, you do not have to cram everything from breakfast to drinks to dessert onto the same menu. Separate menus for different times of day or different courses can reduce distractions for your customers. Also, parents are appreciative of a kid's menu which offers smaller portions at a lower price.

LABEL SPECIAL DISHES

Do you offer vegetarian or vegan meals? What about gluten-free or heart-healthy dishes? Your customers with dietary restrictions will appreciate being able to easily find meals they can eat.

OFFER A VARIETY OF PRICES

Lynton Viñas

A Concise Guide for Operating a Restaurant

Of course it would be great if every customer ordered your most expensive menu item, but you have to provide choices for people with smaller budgets. Try including some sandwiches with your steaks. My husband told me that when he ran a steakhouse, one of his most popular items for children at lunch was a peanut butter and jelly sandwich. Although they could get that at home, they begged for it from their parents, because it was an unusual item for restaurants.

Creating a great restaurant menu does not have to be hard; just keep your customers in mind. By creating a menu that is engaging and easy-to-read while also reflecting your restaurant's brand, you will find that a menu is more than a sales tool. It is representative of your unique brand.

Notice the Simplicity but Elegance of the Following Two Menus

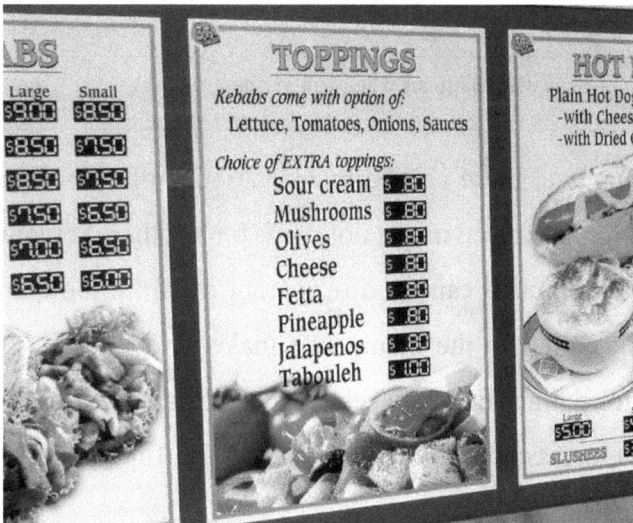

TODAY'S MENU

APPETIZERS

Our menu changes daily, based on the availability of local ingredients.

RUTABAGA AND TOASTED HAZELNUT SOUP — $12
soy roasted hazelnuts, horseradish cream, Challerhocker

MARINATED LOCAL OYSTER MUSHROOM SALAD — $16
pig ear terrine, pickled plum jelly, jerusalem artichoke, Bosc pear with mint, petit greens, red wine mousseline
~ Half portion: $9 ~

DAY BOAT SCALLOPS — $14
fennel, prosciutto, black bean sauce

MAIN ENTRÉES

GRILLED FAROE ISLAND SALMON — $26
quinoa, oyster mushrooms, brussels sprout leaves, beet mustard

PAN ROASTED DUCK BREAST — $29
herbed farro, orange-frisee salad, honey gastrique

CRISPY DUCK IN PORT CHERRY SAUCE — $36
roasted turnips, parsnips, rutabaga and carrots with cornmeal, johnnycake wrapped duck confit, bok choy

TENDERLOIN OF BEEF WELLINGTON — $48
foie gras, spinach, duxelle
~ Add Bearnaise, Red Wine, or Bordelaise sauce for $2 extra ~

Life is what happens when you are busy making other plans.

Of course, there can be many varieties of menus, and what works for one place might not work for another. Sometimes, the unusual approach can set a restaurant off from the competition when it comes to the menu. Just make sure that being unusual does not detract from the real purpose of the menu, which is to provide a succinct, descriptive list of the fine food offered by your restaurant.

A Concise Guide for Operating a Restaurant

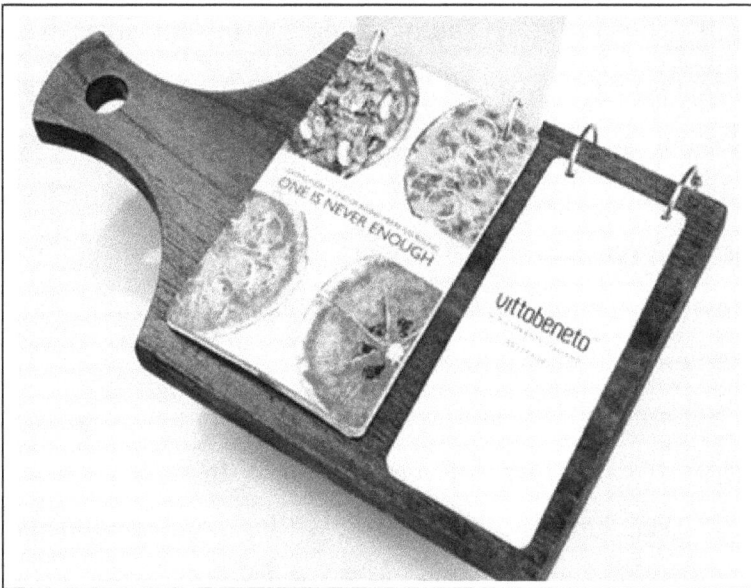

Lynton Viñas

A Concise Guide for Operating a Restaurant

(6) Storage needs: Do you plan to receive lots of small deliveries during the week and have a high turnover of inventory, or do you plan to purchase in bulk for savings and store on-site? Will your distributor let you buy in bulk and store in their warehouse without an additional fee? Do you have a lot of high-value inventory that needs special security measures? This is an example of operational and functional design considerations, which are not part of the typical interior design portfolio. Where design meets function is often a gap for restaurant designers without considerable restaurant industry experience.

(7) Refrigeration: An integral part of any restaurant is its refrigeration systems. Restaurant refrigeration ranges from small coolers (like dorm fridges) to massive walk-in refrigerators and freezers and everything in between. Carefully selecting the right type of refrigeration for a new restaurant will make your commercial kitchen run smoothly and contribute to a positive experience for staff and customers. One of the biggest steps in opening a restaurant is buying the right kind of commercial kitchen equipment.

Before you buy any restaurant refrigeration, you need to decide what types of coolers and freezers you need. Your restaurant concept and size will be the biggest factors in what you buy for restaurant refrigeration. If you have limited

Lynton Viñas

space in your restaurant design, then a large walk-in refrigerator probably will not work. If your menu is based on a lot of frozen foods, like pub grub such as fries, chicken wings and onion rings, then you will need ample freezer space. Your food distributors' delivery schedule will also affect what you need for restaurant refrigeration. Restaurants that receive daily deliveries of fresh meats, seafood and produce will not need as much refrigeration as restaurants that only get a delivery once or twice a week. In some cases, the suppliers will actually supply refrigeration units, but this is becoming rarer now than in the past.

(8) Lighting Design: Lighting can set the mood in a restaurant. Candles are romantic. Soft red or blue lights are serene. Low lighting is relaxing. However, the staff needs task lighting that is bright enough for them to see what they are doing, particularly in the kitchen area. Lighting is a highly specialized area of design. A restaurant without a thoughtfully conceived lighting plan is like flashlight without batteries.

(9) Acoustical Design: A restaurant engages all of the senses. Certainly sight, smell, taste and touch should be considered in restaurant design projects, but what about sound? Is your restaurant best suited for peace and quiet or would it be better suited to have a bar that feels busy and bustling? Music can set the tone and create ambience. Likewise,

no music can also have an impact. For example, many night clubs design areas that make it easy to talk to someone you meet on a dance floor where you could not hear yourself talk with loud music blaring all about.

(10) Aroma Design: Hopefully, the kitchen will emit an aroma which should be pleasant and appealing. This does not happen by accident though. Without proper considerations, you may fill your restaurant with smoke, haze or unpleasant odours. You can also have aroma pollution where there are too many scents floating about. Beyond the aroma of the cuisine, there are other considerations. One restaurant where I worked introduced aromatherapy in a way that stimulated the senses and appetite before customers were even in the dining room. There is nothing worse than smelling dirty mop water in the lobby or an unpleasant bathroom odour. Without smell we would not have taste, so clearly this is an important consideration in restaurant design and should not be overlooked.

(11) Restaurant Design Process: The steps in the restaurant design process can be expanded or collapsed to suit tastes. There are hundreds of inter-dependent decisions and steps. Generally, the timing of these projects can range from several very intense weeks to potentially a year or more for large-scale developments. It is better to spend more time in planning and development with an experienced professional than to rush in to

the design and then try to undo mistakes later. It is much easier to make a change on a digital file than it is to change a major mistake on a completed building. Each country, state, province and city can have dramatically different codes and laws governing design and architecture. As a result, the permitting process for a new project can take from a few weeks to several years. Navigating through this minefield of bureaucracy can be challenging. Ultimately, all restaurant design plans must be submitted to the appropriate authorities. They must be "signed and sealed," meaning a senior licensed architect or city/county/provincial engineer or building inspector has reviewed the design and the mechanical, electrical and plumbing plans. In the realm of design, a licensed designer may submit plans that do not call for significant modifications to an existing building, such as structural changes. In the hierarchy of licensing, a licensed architect can approve anything a licensed designer can, but a licensed designer cannot approve all that a licensed architect can. Just as with conceptual development, with design and architectural planning the location of selected consultants is less important than specialization. This process can and often is completed at a distance. That said, it is often advised for complex projects to also retain a local architect that is familiar with the codes in some jurisdictions and has the relationships to physically walk the plans through permitting.

A Concise Guide for Operating a Restaurant

Although it should not be the case, the local consultants sometimes do get some special treatment and dispensations.

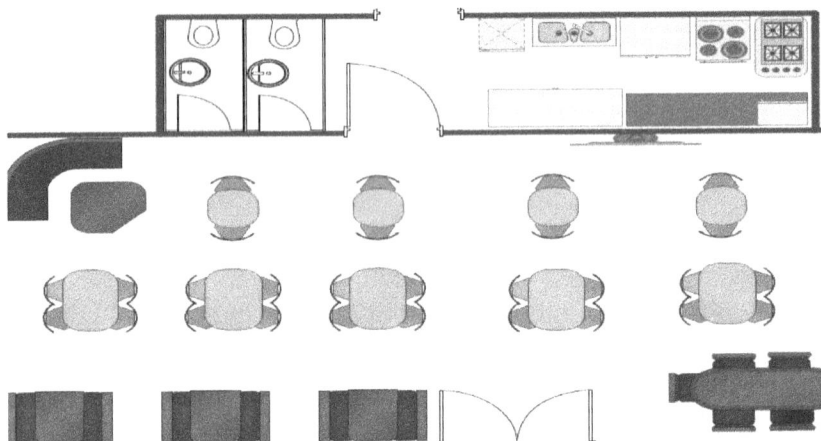

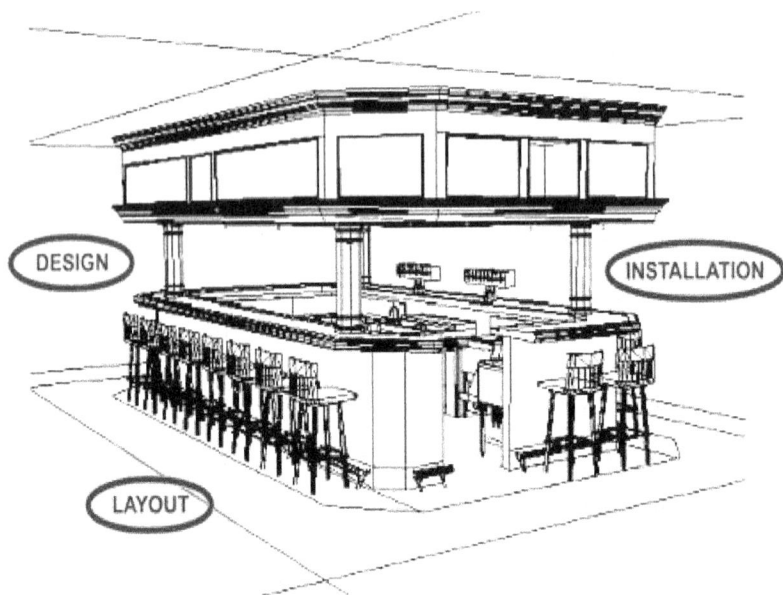

A Concise Guide for Operating a Restaurant

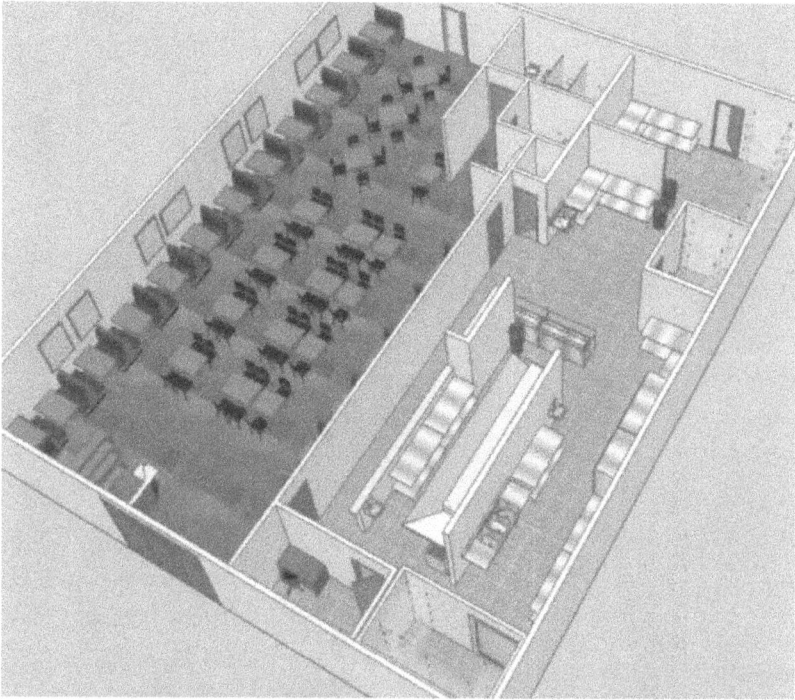

(12) Signage: This is an expensive item, but it is the first thing customers see, so it must be highly visible and original. This includes more than just the outdoor sign. It includes easels, posted boards, and as mentioned earlier, even bathroom signs.

Bigger is Better

Keep your restaurant sign tall and large so it can be spotted by those walking or driving by. If you are located in a tourist-heavy area, consider investing in billboards, roadside signs, or car top signs to pique the interest of hungry travelers. Be sure to include easy directions on your billboard or roadside sign that even an out-of-towner can follow.

Lynton Viñas

A Concise Guide for Operating a Restaurant

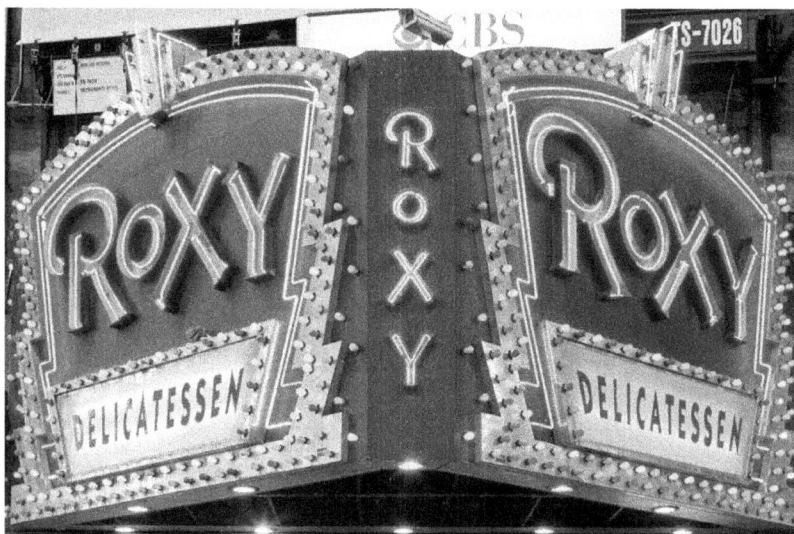

Consider Alternate Views

An A-frame sidewalk sign is great for those walking by, but if you are at a busy roadside area cars will block the view to customers walking across the street. Trees and even curb-side plants can obstruct views as well. Consider placing another form of signage at eye-level height or higher on your windows, awning or rooftop. And if you are located on a corner, do not forget to work all angles. Be sure to comply with local regulations regarding fire codes and blocking rooftop views.

Work with the Space You Have

If your storefront does not lend itself to signs, consider other creative routes. Use colourful markers on your windows. Place a memorable and iconic object in front of your restaurant such as a mascot, unique landscape, an unusual lamp or a rooftop decoration. Paint your awning, entrance steps and other architecture accouterments with eye-catching colours and an appealing design.

Advertise Day and Night

Marketing does not stop when the sun goes down. Purchase a lighted sign to advertise your restaurant when it is dark and even after closing. LED signs glow brighter than traditional lights, yet can still be seen in direct sunlight and behind glass windows. Plus, they use half the energy of standard neon signs, and are safer because they do not have a high voltage transformer. If you do not use a lighted sign, be sure to illuminate signage with overhead lighting.

Use Animation and Action

Catch customer attention with a sign that moves. Today's technologies allow for programmable signs that have scrolling messages. Many lighted signs offer multiple display modes that prompt text to blink, flash or crawl. Even a basic swinging sign or hanging porch signs draws more attention that a standard stationary sign.

Say It and Show It

Let your products do the talking. Use window space to advertise freshly made bread loaves, bakery displays or even show meals being made.

Keep Text Short, Simple and Savoury

A Concise Guide for Operating a Restaurant

Use words sparingly: The industry average for reading a billboard is six seconds, so keep your message under 10 words if your sign is aimed at catching the attention of drivers and those quickly walking by.

Humour Them

A little humour can go a long way when it comes to attracting diners. Assess your crowd and choose the best variety of comedy, whether that humour is self-deprecating, food-pun related or even a bit cheesy. However, be very careful about double entendres as some people are easily offended.

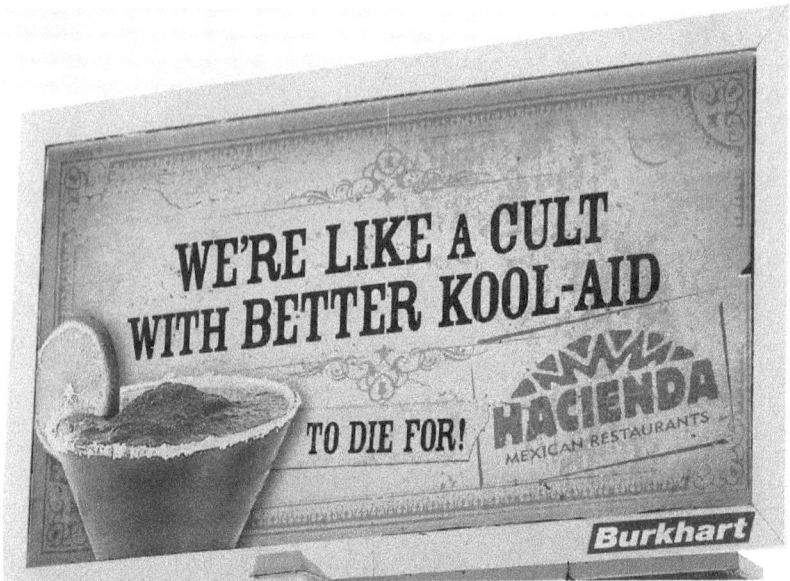

A Concise Guide for Operating a Restaurant

Do Not Underestimate Nostalgia

If you are looking to stand out among a row of restaurants, *"Family Owned and Operated Since 1928"* can speak volumes more than *"$3 Hot Dogs."* Sentimental text could be the factor that helps you beat out nearby competition.

Utilize Social Media

A simple tag like *"Follow us on Facebook at Lynton's Gourmet Burgers"* allows customers to easily check your restaurant on smart phones as they walk by. Post your unique restaurant signs on Facebook, Twitter and Instagram to catch the attention of those following you.

Brand

Choose a few signature elements and work them into your signage. Make sure your restaurant logo is an easy to recognize design. Prominently display your logo outside the restaurant. Choose a signature colour scheme and be consistent in your use of it. Windows, menus and even outdoor table umbrellas are all fair game for displaying text and logos.

Post an Easy-to-Read Outdoor Menu

The last thing you want to do is lose a potential diner because your menu is not easily accessible. Post a free standing menu holder in an easy-to-read location for those passing by. If space does not allow for a full menu, promote signature dishes near your restaurant entrance to at least give customers a taste of what you offer. Promote a daily item - such as *"Fresh Catch of the Day"* or *"Soup du Jour"* to create an impulsive only available today opportunity for diners. It does not hurt to have a few traditional favourites on display for less adventurous diners. Check out menu psychology resources on line for more tips and tricks to write the best menu. For example: Do not use currency signs, as according to research, diners spend significantly more on menus without them.

Chapter 3

Deciding on Location and Whether to Rent or Buy

Location can make or break a restaurant. Finding the perfect location is a time consuming and tedious process. Do not rush this decision. It is the most important one that you will make. Wait until you have several prospective properties and then weigh the options carefully. Remember, once you sign the lease and open your restaurant, the one thing that is almost impossible to change is your location. You need to consider the following factors when choosing a location:

- Visibility and passing traffic (foot and car)
- Parking
- Demographics
- Potential for outdoor seating
- Zoning
- Refurbishment required
- Freehold or leasehold
- Competition
- Complementary businesses located close by

Do not just get statistics from the normal sources or the last census. Pound the pavement, check pricing, service, style and find out when others establishments are busy. Are there enough potential customers in the specific segment you are targeting to ensure you get your own share?

Finally do not be afraid to open right next door to your competitors. For example, if you are selling hamburgers, why not open across the street from McDonald's? They spend nearly one billion dollars a year world-wide on advertising. Dave Thomas of Wendy's fame, in his initial stages, always tried to get close to McDonald's with his new restaurants because he felt his hamburgers were bigger and juicer; therefore, people would naturally be attracted to his places just to try them out, even though they were slightly more expensive. The formula worked well for him.

A Concise Guide for Operating a Restaurant

In most books on business the authors say it is best to stay as far away from your competitors as possible. However, in the restaurant business it is often best to stay as close as possible to your competitors, as your potential customers may have already decided that they are coming to a certain part of town to eat. Have you ever noticed the tendency for car dealers, for example, to all congregate in one area, which makes shopping easier for the consumer. The same technique can be applied to restaurants.

Should you buy or lease a location? For the new restaurant owner, the investment necessary to buy a property may be the deciding factor in this question. Buying a location is a major and typically a long term commitment usually reserved for someone who has significant resources. The advantage to leasing is that it provides an opportunity to begin on a smaller budget. It may also offer an easier exit strategy if things do not work out. The major advantage to owning a location is that you will not have to worry about a rent hike, although municipalities/states/provinces will reappraise the property every year, so the taxes will continuously go up; however, businesses usually get a preferential rate over homeowners as the politicians prefer to tax working men and women more excessively than businesses. In addition, as an owner you do not have to work within the parameters set up by a landlord, giving you more freedom to do as wished with the property. The final consideration when buying any real estate is the projected value of the property. Will the price of the property appreciate or depreciate in the coming years? While the goal of most restaurant owners is to build a successful eatery, in the past the acquisition of prime real estate has made ownership very rewarding. In fact, sometimes appreciation makes it more feasible to sell than to continue to operate.

Practicalities of Renting a Place

Before renting a location, it is critical to consult with property experts. A business realtor will be able to advise on the best deal to suit your business needs and a solicitor (attorney) will be able to advise on legal points arising from the lease, as well as the agreement between you and the landlord. Think carefully before signing any agreement. Do not sign anything unless you completely understand it and agree with it. Here are some of the things you will need to think about:

(1) The actual cost of renting, including any ancillaries must be considered. Be careful of the proverbial hidden clauses in contracts.

(2) Be aware not only what the rent will be when the lease begins, but how much it could go up over the term. There are usually escalator clauses in all leases, and if you are in a mall, there is usually a percentage of gross sales that kicks in after

you reach a certain level of revenue. Some malls are littered with vacant stores because people go out of business but must still pay rent.

(3) The length of the lease is important as you need to consider how long you want to commit yourself to renting the premises. Remember that unless your landlord agrees that you can give up your lease or transfer it to someone else you will have to pay rent for the whole period of the lease, even if your income dries up. Leases typically have agreements of between one and 25 years. Do not lock yourself into a long lease, at least not the first few years that you are in business. If your restaurant fails you do not want to be locked into years of rent that you cannot afford to pay.

(4) Quitting decisions often come into play, not because of failure, but because of circumstances (deaths, spouses getting a job in a different place, other family or personal issues) that necessitate closing a business. How easily could you give up renting if you no longer need your premises for a variety of reasons or run into financial difficulties? Will you be able to transfer the premises to someone else? Will the landlord allow you to give a lease up? Do you have the opportunity to break (end the lease) at certain intervals. Putting in a break clause would allow you to choose whether or not to continue renting the property.

A Concise Guide for Operating a Restaurant

(5) Insurance is an important consideration. The landlord may expect you to insure the premises yourself or to pay for the insurance that the landlord carries.

(6) Repairs are a fact of life, whether in the restaurant or some other business. Are building repairs included in the rent? If you make significant repairs to the plumbing or heating, then ask if they can be deducted from your regular rent. Most landlords would rather give free or reduced rent one month than shell out cash to make repairs.

(7) Service charges can add considerably to expenses. On top of the rent, the landlord may charge more for services such as cleaning, heating and lighting. These may be more expensive than providing them yourself.

(8) Guarantees may be required, especially in a long term lease. The landlord may ask you for a financial guarantee, or may ask you to provide a guarantee for anyone who takes over your lease. If things go wrong, a personal guarantee could bankrupt you.

(9) Protection when the lease ends is important. Will you have the right to renew the lease when it comes to an end? If a landlord sees a business is successful, he or she may want to increase the rent an exorbitant amount. For this reason, it may be advisable to include a guarantee renewal option at a set percentage increase.

Lynton Viñas

A Concise Guide for Operating a Restaurant

(10) Restrictions imposed by the local authority or the landlord may an adverse effect on the business (delivery or loading times, rubbish disposal, parking, noise, lighting, litter, etc. Also, does the premises have an existing licence to sell alcohol?

(11) The landlord's reputation should be researched. Is he or she someone you want to have a working relationship with? Is there a history of problems? Seek out former tenants and find out what their experiences with the landlord were.

(12) The history of the property should be researched. Find out whether any businesses have failed there and why. Sometimes a long list of failures attaches a stigma to a place. Was the property a restaurant before? Ask neighbouring tenants for their input. Will the space work for a restaurant? Is there suitable ventilation, services, power, etc? Finally before renting a property, make sure you can get planning permission to make any changes you need to make. Some buildings have restrictions on what can be done, so this can be important.

(13) Associated with start up costs is finding reliable suppliers. Try and negotiate credit terms so you are not always paying for your products up front.

(14) Designing your restaurant is an important consideration related to location. If you have the budget, use an interior designer. Make sure they have experience designing restaurants

and have a portfolio of their work to show. Emphasize to your interior designer the need to adhere to your budget and that your restaurant should have curb appeal.

Create a design that facilitates the movements of employees in and out of the kitchen. This will help create seamless service. The public likes to see who is preparing their meals, so many restaurants have an open kitchen, but this does not mean the general prep area must be exposed. This type of design also brings chefs out of the kitchen and some of them are real artists who have a flair for showmanship in preparation of food. So, location can mean more than just the physical location itself, it can be the location of areas in the restaurant for maximum efficiency and eye appeal.

A Concise Guide for Operating a Restaurant

Never under estimate the viability of a location. What might seem unworkable could, with some adjustments, be very effective if some innovation is used.

Sometimes it is advisable to be among your competition.

Innovative and creative exterior design can create interest.

Lynton Viñas

A Concise Guide for Operating a Restaurant

Exterior design may get customers in the first time, but good food and stellar service are what keeps them coming back.

Classic marrying of design with the locality (New Orleans here) can make a restaurant part of the neighbourhood and develop a genuine mystique. This restaurant has done that since 1840.

A Concise Guide for Operating a Restaurant

Sometimes the exterior design is of no consequence as evidenced by Pink's Hot Dogs on La Brea Avenue in Hollywood. This tiny little place has been around since 1939 and does nearly three million dollars a year in sales. Deliver a superior product with a smile and customer loyalty is assured.

Chapter 4

Start Up Costs

What are the costs involved in setting up a restaurant? There is absolutely no concrete answer to this question as each restaurant operation is different. Obviously, costs are going to be more in a large metropolitan area as opposed to a small village. However, there are some specifics that can apply in general. The following start up costs are common in most situations.

• Obtaining a lease and professional fees

A Concise Guide for Operating a Restaurant

• Premises remodel

• Kitchen fit out, ovens, refrigeration etc

• Staff recruitment and uniforms

• Furniture, crockery, table cloths, flowers, pictures, etc.

 • Signage

• Initial stock of food

• Launch marketing fund

• Working capital

Remember there are also a multitude of hidden expenses that will crop up unexpectedly as times goes on, so have some funds (the more the better) set aside for these emergencies. At least six months of working capital is highly recommended. The majority of all businesses, including restaurants, fail because they are generally under-capitalized. In fact, countless numbers of people lose all they have. Many restaurant owners wind up asking themselves why they spent money on things that were not needed. So be very frugal in all matters.

Equipment and Fit Out?

Buying the kitchen equipment and fitting out a restaurant will probably be the biggest expense. Look into buying second hand equipment, if feasible. You may find that another entrepreneur's misfortune will contribute to your success. Recently failed restaurants probably generally leave owners in dire financial straits.

Lynton Viñas

A Concise Guide for Operating a Restaurant

One way that these entrepreneurs recover a loss is to dump their equipment quickly, often for far less than they paid for it. This is the downside of capitalism – one person's failure can be another person's success. Also, remember to buy only what is needed, because even a good deal is not good if you can get by without the equipment.

Look in the newspaper and online at classified ad sites to find where these sell-offs are occurring. Also, it is sometimes possible to get free equipment or equipment on loan from suppliers? Freezers and refrigeration units are often available for free in the right circumstances as are items like coffee makers if you buy from a specific supplier. However, be aware free equipment may not be completely free as you may have to agree to stay with a certain supplier for a set period of time. Therefore, free equipment is often incorporated into the long agreement, but it is often worth it as it frees up capital for other things.

Raising Capital

Most entrepreneurs find this the most daunting task in opening a restaurant. If we all had money, most of us would be successful businesspersons, but that is not the way of a world where the privileged get all the benefits. Still, for those of us born to modest means, there are a number of potential sources for raising funds.

A Concise Guide for Operating a Restaurant

(1) *Savings:* Not everybody has savings but if you do, this is a good place to start. Many people also have equity in a home, and a line of credit with that home as collateral is relatively easy to obtain. After all, banks make money if you succeed by lending you money, and if you fail they wind up with your home. As author Wayne Frye once said, "Bankers steal more with the stroke of a pen than a robber steals with a gun. This is the way of a world where the real thieves escape justice."

(2) *Get frugal with money and time*. If you do not have savings yet or a home, now is a good time to start putting money away. Your timeline for starting your business may be six months to a year or more, so if you start putting money away now, you will have at least a starting point from which to raise more cash. Starting a business is about sacrifice and that often means adjusting to a more frugal lifestyle.

(3) Convincing lenders is a way to raise money. For you to be able to borrow money from a bank you will need to convince them that the business is viable and that it can pay any interest and make the principle repayments as they fall due. Many times it is possible to get an interest only loan so that each month you simply pay interest on the principle. The bank will also look for some kind of security for any loan. Once the business is set up, an overdraft can usually be arranged, although it should only be taken out as part of a tightly controlled cash flow plan.

Lynton Viñas

A Concise Guide for Operating a Restaurant

(5) *Friends and family* are sources of capital, but, in my humble opinion, this should usually be the last resort unless you have a billionaire uncle. Borrowing from family can create hardships for them as they want to be helpful, but may not be able to ride out a long drought without repayment, and personal problems can pop up in their lives which might make them need immediate or partial repayment. There are a number of additional pitfalls associated with borrowing from friends and family; on the positive side, such borrowing arrangements can often be made on more attractive terms than might otherwise be available from a more formal source of funding. For example, it may be possible to borrow either without any form of security against the loan and it may also be possible to borrow at either a lower rate of interest, or even interest free. Repayments may also be possible over an extended period of time and a detailed business plan may not be necessary. It is best to keep any arrangement formal, however, and to give the benefactor as much financial information as possible upfront. You will be responsible for their money, and as such; it is in everyone's interest to manage the money effectively.

(6) *Venture Capitalists*: People with money always want to make more money. The cycle of greed simply means that most people can never have enough. The Cree word for it is Keshagesh (greedy guts), which refers to those who never have

enough, no matter how rich they might be. Many of these people pool their money in venture capital firms that are looking for small businesses to invest in. If you are simply looking to run a sweet little bistro, the best you could hope for would probably be a local businessperson who is keen to invest. But if you are looking to launch a new concept restaurant with potential for rapid expansion, venture capital funding may be available. If you choose a venture capitalist, make sure you maintain control of running your business.

(5) *Writing a Business Plan*: Trying to convince anyone, either a bank manager or venture capitalist, to lend you the money to embark on your scheme is going to take more than a hazy idea sketched on the back of a napkin. You need to be prepared with a business plan, a presentation of your idea of how the business will work with a realistic breakdown of costs and expected revenue. Only then will any investor take you seriously. The business plan will include:

• Start up costs

• Fixed and variable operating costs (Rent is fixed, staff costs are variable)

• Forecasted average spending (include best and worst case scenarios)

• Analysis of the likely gross profit on food and wine and any ancillary sales

A Concise Guide for Operating a Restaurant

• Analysis of your likely breakeven point

• A marketing and sales plan

• A plan for the source of funding

• A budgeted monthly profit and loss statement along with a performance and forecasted cash flow analysis.

A business plan is also vital in securing enterprise grants, investments and loans, which you may need when starting your business. For example, in many countries the government will lend the money or guarantee it, especially for underserved populations.

Compiling your business plan can seem like the most difficult and the least exciting part of starting a new business, but it really is imperative as without a plan everything is simply hit and miss.

(6) *Deciding on a legal structure for your restaurant:* In most countries there are three types of businesses that you need to be concerned with: sole proprietorship, partnership and limited company (corporation). A sole proprietorship operates exactly as the name suggests. You are actually trading in your own name. Even though you might call the business something completely different from your own name, your name will be on all official documentation. A partnership has the same set up as a sole proprietorship, except that you have equal responsibility for the business with your partner or partners. If you are in a

partnership it is wise to draw up a legal partnership agreement to ensure that all partners know where they stand. This is also very useful if you close the business. Many businesses decide to register as a limited company (corporation) once they reach a certain level of turnover to take advantage of limited liability status. This is because the major drawback of being a sole proprietorship or partnership is that you are personally responsible for any business debts if the company closes down. These debts are treated the same as personal debts, and any personal assets (such as your house) could be claimed to effectuate repayment.

Limited companies have directors and shareholders. In most countries, there must be a minimum of 2 directors and one company secretary (who can also be a director) who is responsible for submitting the company accounts to the proper governmental authorities. However a limited company is separate from the directors and shareholders who may not be held personally responsible for any debts if the company becomes insolvent. Unlike a sole proprietorship, where your income is effectively the same as your salary, as a director you can pay yourself a salary from the turnover of the business or you can take no salary and just declare yourself a dividend (depending on the country where you do business) and also the company, itself, must pay separate income tax. As a limited company there are various legal requirements you must adhere to for which a fine or penalty is payable if they are not complied with. These include employment laws, and depending on the country, working tax credit, maternity leave, statutory sick pay, employer's liability insurance, tax laws, workers' compensation insurance, tax laws, health and safety laws etc. It is apparent that regardless of how you set-up your business, there is a lot of administrative work involved with running a business.

If you are not sure which legal structure would best suit your business, you can get advice from an accountant or solicitor (lawyer).

Registering your restaurant with the health department is a must. You cannot open your doors until you are inspected.

Before opening, get in touch with your local authorities to plan your business, organize waste and recycling collection and get appropriate training and tools. You will also need a specific license if you want to do the following things:

• Sell or supply alcohol
• Provide entertainment, such as theatre, cinema or live music
• Sell food from a stall or van on the street

If you have created a specific, unique image for your business you can register for trademark protection to keep it from being used by competitors and other interested parties. A trademark can protect your business's name, slogan, domain name, logo, colour or sound, but only if it is distinctive for that business within its class (industry type). You are not required by law in most countries to register your trademark, however it is wise to do so to ensure no one else can copy it or use it for their own gain.

When starting a restaurant, insurance is a necessity. Here is a quick review of the essential and optional insurance that you will need to consider.

(1) Public liability insurance will cover the cost of a claim if a customer in your restaurant is injured or killed, or if their property is damaged while on the premises. Injuries are infrequent, but they do occur.

(2) Building insurance is necessary if you own the building, and sometimes even renters are required to have building insurance or pay the owner for the coverage. (If you rent, be sure the owner has the right insurance amount and types of specific coverage needed.)

(3) Employers' liability insurance is required by law to cover your employees. It will pay the cost of a claim from an employee who has been injured at work, or who has become seriously ill as a result of working for you. Employer's liability insurance may seem like a nuisance and unnecessary extra expense, but the law is there to protect you and your business. If an employee is injured or becomes ill in the course of their

work, and it can be proven as your fault, you could face a claim for compensation. This policy will ensure that your business and you are protected.

(4) Contents insurance covers you against a wide range of perils and disasters such as fire, theft or water damage.

(5) Business interruption insurance compensates your business for lost income when it is forced to close due to an event that is stated in your policy. It could be for an incident as small as a power outage lasting a couple of days that prevents your restaurant from opening, or one as big as a fire on your premises which could prevent your business from opening for weeks or months. Thanks to the internet, it is now possible to compare multiple policies and providers of public liability coverage in a similar way to car and home insurance. Although the choice of companies is much more limited, online business insurance comparison sites offer price and policy comparison services for most types and size of business. Never ever be under insured!

What tax will you need to pay? Over a year, a business owner has to make certain reports (returns) and payments to various government bodies. Value Added Tax (VAT) is a tax businesses charge when they supply their goods and services in most countries. The USA is notably one of the few nations without this tax which is generally used to provide social amenities to citizens, which may explain the dearth of social amenities there.

If you are employing other people, you will need to work out and pay your employees' tax and National Insurance (sometimes referred to as Social Insurance or Social Security) contributions. These come out of the wages you pay, but in most countries employers must match what the employee contributes. Remember, you need to keep a record of everything you pay your employees, including wages, other payments or bonuses and benefits. You also need to make sure that you adhere to employment law on issues such as employee rights, working hours, minimum wages and equal opportunities. As an employer, you will have to deduct these taxes and send payment to the proper government authorities.

As a business you can claim tax advantages called capital allowances on certain purchases or investments. This means you can deduct a portion of these costs from your taxable profits and reduce your tax bill. If bookkeeping and pay roll is new to you, consider taking a course to learn the basics, or even better, if you can afford it, hire an accountant.

There are national restaurant associations in most countries that represent and lobby for restaurant owners. It might be advisable to join as they also offer all types of training and business assistance.

Chapter 5

Cash Flow Management

The managing of the accounts is important for the survival of any business. Thus, the proper management of the cash flow as it relates to receipts and payments from the company account will help to improve the financial management system. Also, the management of the books in terms of cash and bank accounts with bank reconciliation will serve as a guide for proper financial flow. Managing cash is the lifeblood of your business. Managed well, your company remains strong.

A Concise Guide for Operating a Restaurant

Managed poorly, your business goes into cardiac arrest. If you haven't considered cash management an important issue, then you are probably undermining your restaurant's short-term stability and its long-term survival.

How can you manage business cash better? Start with understanding how good cash-management practices can affect your company's growth and survival. You must be able to accurately assess your current cash position and get fairly reliable predictions at key intervals about how much you will need to meet the company's expenses. So, let us take a look at cash flow analysis by categorizing it.

What is cash flow? In financial accounting, a cash flow statement, also known as statement of cash flows or funds flow statement is a financial statement that shows how changes in balance sheet accounts and income affect cash and cash equivalents, and breaks the analysis down to operating, investing and financing activities. Essentially, the cash flow statement is concerned with the flow of cash in and cash out of the business. The statement captures both the current operating results and the accompanying changes in the balance sheet. As an analytical tool, the statement of cash flows is useful in determining the short-term viability of a company, particularly its ability to pay bills. People and groups interested in cash flow statements include:

A Concise Guide for Operating a Restaurant

• Accounting personnel who want to know whether the organization will be able to cover payroll and other actual expenses.

• Potential lenders or creditors, who want a clear picture of a company's ability to repay.

• Potential investors, who want to evaluate whether the company is financially sound.

• Potential employees or contractors, who want to know whether the company will be able to provide expected compensation.

• Shareholders of the business if it is a corporation, as the cash flow statement reflects a firm's liquidity.

The balance sheet is a snapshot of a firm's financial resources and obligations at a single point in time, and the income statement summarizes a firm's financial transactions over an interval of time. These two financial statements reflect the accrual basis accounting used by firms to match revenues with the expenses associated with generating those revenues. The cash flow statement includes only inflows and outflows of cash and cash equivalents; it excludes transactions that do not directly affect cash receipts and payments. These considerable non-cash transactions include things like depreciation on various items and/or write-offs on bad debts or credit losses to name just a few.

A Concise Guide for Operating a Restaurant

The cash flow statement is a cash basis report on three types of financial activities: operating activities, investing activities and financing activities. Non-cash activities are usually reported in footnotes. The cash flow statement is intended to:

• Provide information on a firm's liquidity and solvency and its ability to change cash flows in future circumstances.

• Provide additional information for evaluating changes in assets, liabilities and equity.

• Improve the comparability of different firms' operating performance by eliminating the effects of different accounting methods.

• Indicate the amount, timing and likelihood of future cash flows.

The cash flow statement has been adopted as a standard financial statement because it eliminates allocations, which might be derived from different accounting methods, such as various timeframes for depreciating fixed assets.

In the most general sense, cash flow for a business is simply the flow of cash through the organization over time. Cash flows are needed for the firm to survive and thrive. Cash is paid out in return for the inputs that are used in the process of building worth, such as materials, labour and professional service after goods or services are created and sold. Cash flows that are not reinvested in the production and sales process may be paid out to owners. For the restaurant, investments in various business projects provide future cash flows that contribute to the firm's economic value. An understanding of how future cash flows are generated and what factors affect those flows is an integral part of making decisions that increase a firm's economic value and long range survivability.

This is not meant to be too technical, but the truth is that without rudimentary knowledge of finance your restaurant is headed for trouble. He or she who is not prepared to deal with finances is simply in the wrong business.

Being the owner or manager of a restaurant is not an easy task. It entails far more than just throwing your doors open and waiting for customers to flock in. If it was that easy, there would be a lot more restaurants in the world. Look around and see how many restaurants come and go over the years. Failures are around 60% at five years, and many cannot even last five years. So, every single thing covered in this concise manual is meant to improve your chances of success. I have, fortunately, never been involved with a failed restaurant, but I do know that working, managing and owning one is a daunting task that requires great dedication and no small measure of patience and diligence.

My husband had two successful restaurants in Myrtle Beach, South Carolina, but after a few years he decided that the excellent financial rewards were not adding to his family's quality of life, so he moved on. This guide is meant to not only make the reader a success at managing or owning a restaurant, but also to make sure that he or she is well aware of the amount of time and energy that must go into making a restaurant a success.

Chapter 6

Importance of Company Buy-In to the Marketing Function

There are many disciplines that have to come together to complete a successful new restaurant prototype. There are literally thousands of decisions that must be made through the course of a restaurant design project. All of these decisions should be viewed through the lens of the brand and that is where the domain of marketing becomes so important in making sure the venture is a success. I am not a licensed designer or architect, but I do know that these two functions are critical to the success of a new restaurant. I also know that ultimately, everything done is part of the marketing function.

Now, how could accounting be part of the marketing function? How could sweeping the floor be part of the marketing function, and what about the chef, the kitchen staff, the wait staff, the bartender, the hostess, etc? The answer is pretty simple – if they do not function in sync with the brand idea, then the chain is broken and the link which is missing can have an adverse effect on marketing the restaurant. The person who sweeps the floor is part of the marketing function, because that clean floor projects the brand image. Ditto for every single job that is part of an actual living restaurant organism into which each individual person breathes life.

Restaurant design is not just about picking colours and fabrics, signage, uniforms and a host of other things. It involves a lot of technical knowledge of how restaurants work, operational considerations and how everything ultimately relates to the marketing function which promotes the brand. .Great restaurant design is complicated, because ultimately it is what you are marketing to customers. It is an ideal that is projecting the image that says to the public that this is a place where I want to dine. That is why shopping for the cheapest is not always the best approach. Look at the effectiveness before ever committing to hiring anyone.

A Concise Guide for Operating a Restaurant

As alluded to earlier, I have a husband who was once coined a marketing genius, but that was over 20 years ago and it was not in reference to restaurants but to promoting hockey teams and motion pictures, and if I am going to hire a marketing consultant for my restaurant, I would obviously listen to my husband, but ultimately his ideas are probably antiquated, because he has not been in the restaurant business in many years. Yes, his ideas on marketing in general may be valid, but I would, after massaging his ego, seek out someone with recent experience in marketing restaurants, and if I cannot afford a marketing consultant I will read about successes in marketing restaurants for ideas. My husband also told me, "In marketing you are only as good as your last promotion." His mystery novels sell well, and he was once a best-selling textbook author in regards to marketing. Still, that was long ago, and I am sure even he would say with feigned modesty, "You need someone who has promoted restaurants recently, not a mind that has been devoted to coining novels with violence, sex, murder and mayhem."

The key to success is not just devotion to being a success, but devotion to the idea that everything ultimately reverts back to branding, which is what marketing is all about, and how that brand can be effectively promoted to a public that has many choices and can be extremely fickle.

A Concise Guide for Operating a Restaurant

With the advent of the Internet, the customer base, about half of whom can not remember a time before Google, restaurants need promotions that do more than just get guests through the door. It is about more than a nice atmosphere and great food. To succeed today, it is imperative that restaurants engage directly with guests and make them feel as if they are investing in something, rather than just buying a product. Part of this engagement is making sure that every employee in the restaurant feels part of the team. In fact, the term employee has been replaced by the term associate so each individual feels part of the company, rather than just being an employee. A smart restaurateur promotes this idea. Many times a share of the profits are set aside to use as bonuses to employees, as nothing in the capitalist world speaks louder than cash in motivating people. This is not only good marketing to your employees, but promotes the restaurant to the general public through word-of-mouth as being a company that cares about its workers. Frankly, I prefer dining in a place where I know the workers are being treated with respect and shown appreciation for their efforts.

Lynton Viñas

Chapter 7

Successful Restaurant Promotion

I once told my husband, "Give me a book on brain surgery and I can learn how to perform brain surgery."

My husband replied, "You are a smart woman, and I believe you could probably do it after reading the book, but if I need brain surgery, I prefer someone with a bit more experience than you."

Starting a restaurant is not easy. In the above example, my husband wanted someone with experience, and as alluded to earlier it is highly advisable that before starting a restaurant you should work for period of time in one to develop expertise. A brain surgeon does not just come out of school and start performing brain surgery. He or she has to serve a residency, working with skilled brain surgeons to learn first hand the proper procedures. In the restaurant business, you are going to be a culinary surgeon, so it is advisable you serve an internship or residency in a restaurant.

I went to the Cambridge School of Law, but I never practiced law. Rather, I became a businesswoman who was a trouble-shooting manager for a 200 unit spa corporation. I know the spa business, and spent over ten years perfecting my skills, which range from sweeping the floor to planning a marketing campaign. However, my dream was to work in the hospitality field, so I did not open a restaurant or hotel, but rather went to the International Hotel School in Cape Town, South Africa. I selected that school, because internships are an integral part of the programme. Consequently, I did not just study kitchen management; I did it. I did not just study housekeeping management; I did it. I did not just study restaurant management; I did it. I did not just study front office operations; I did it. What you learn in the classroom is valuable, but the real learning is when you put that acquired knowledge to use in practical situations.

A Concise Guide for Operating a Restaurant

Marketing success is based upon careful planning and putting all the elements together in a coordinated effort that elevates your restaurant above the norm. Every actor wants to play Broadway or see his or her name in bold letters on the movie screen. Every opera singer wants to play the Met, and you, my reader, want to open a restaurant. Well, saddle up your horse and get ready for the ride of your life, because the unfortunate reality is, the food is only about 25% of the restaurant success equation. Yes, the food needs to be fabulous. But, you must remember, restaurants are businesses first and food is merely the product for sale. You need to know how to run a business first, before you start slinging that hash all over town and causing a sensation with your endeavour. That is where marketing comes in, and remember that no matter how good your marketing is, if your product is terrible, then nothing will save you.

Now, let's suppose you have that good product down to a science, and like that brain surgeon you have prepared for this with meticulous precision. Still, none of that is any good without a solid marketing plan to motivate people to walk through those doors into your castle of culinary delight.

Restaurant marketing is not the same as it once was. It is critical that restaurants embrace Internet marketing and cultivate a presence online. While "online" is the theme for many of the restaurant marketing tips from Vision Advertising listed in this chapter, there is still much you can (and should) do offline to promote your business.

Restaurants do not use the yellow pages as much as they used to, and for good reason, as people have moved to the Internet to find what they are looking for. In my opinion, Yellow Page advertising is pretty much nothing more than throwing your money away in today's marketplace. People rely on search engines and consumer review sites to find local restaurants and decide where they want to dine. They want to see the restaurant's menu before visiting and they favour those that have a strong online presence over those that have not embraced the Internet.

As a restaurant owner or manager, you need more than traditional advertising and word of mouth marketing. By all means do not skip those methods, but do take advantage of all the opportunities that the Internet presents. Do a Google search for your type of restaurant and location to see what results show up. If you are already open, where do you rank? Do you even make it to the first page? Considering your competition, will potential diners choose your restaurant from that search? Rather than giving your competitors all the business, think of ways you can market your restaurant online more effectively, because that is, as the saying goes, "Where the action is."

A Concise Guide for Operating a Restaurant

So, with Vision Advertising in mind, let's take a look at how to effectively market your restaurant.

Stay current: Keep yourself up to date on current statistics, trends, facts and figures that can help you analyze your restaurant marketing plan. Should you make any tweaks to how you market your restaurant? Should you position your restaurant differently?

Have a functional website: Can local customers find your restaurant online? Make sure they can with a well-optimized website that does what you want it to do. The key is to get them to your website before they find your competitors. You can create a food blog, list daily specials and direct visitors to your social media profiles and online review sites.

Engage in SEO (Search Engine Optimization) practices: Websites are not just for big companies; now more than ever, small local businesses are realizing the importance of having a website and implementing an Internet marketing strategy. Since 75% of all searches are related to a search for local content, you should be sure that your website will show up for those searches relevant to your restaurant.

Enlist local food bloggers: Ask local food bloggers to review your restaurant in return for a free meal. The outside link will help with rankings, and the positive review will help your reputation.

Monitor review sites: You live or die on your reputation, so pay close attention to what people are saying about your restaurant online. This is where your offline visitors can tell the online world about their (hopefully positive) experience at your restaurant. Thank visitors for positive reviews and respond to and respectfully resolve negative reviews.

Use an online restaurant reservation tool: Invite your customers to make a reservation on-line. You need an online restaurant reservation tool to make it easier for your customers and easier on yourself. And sometimes people just do not want to pick up the phone. They had rather make their reservation in just a few clicks.

Grow your e-mail database: When compared to direct marketing, e-mail marketing is more efficient, environmentally friendly, cheaper and a faster way to keep your customers in the know. Promote your e-newsletters through social media, on your website and inside your restaurant.

Get a social media presence: Strengthen your word of mouth marketing with an interesting, interactive social media presence. This gives you the ability to engage your customers 365 days a year, represent your brand and enlist customers to share their stories.

Do not disregard anything too quickly: The online world is always changing, so it is important to keep your eye out for new marketing ventures that have the potential to stick around awhile. Foursquare, for example, is not as well-known as Facebook, but that does not mean there is not ample marketing opportunities for restaurants. This social platform enables restaurants to offer a variety of deals (for free) that users must check-in to take advantage of. This, along with the fact that users can earn credits for checking-in so many times, makes Foursquare a viable marketing option for restaurants. No matter how innocuous a site might seem, if it is free, use it.

Provide enough incentive for people to pay attention: Give your patrons incentive to follow you on social media channels or to come into your restaurant, and make it simple for them to do so. Put your restaurant specials on Facebook. It is a good idea to have a section where your menu is continuously displayed with specials highlighted.

Run contests: This is a great way to reward social media fans, grow your fan base, bring in more customers and promote loyalty. Give customers a chance to win a great prize and you will give them another reason to come back again. Remember that you can also get other businesses to participate who want to get their name before the public. For example, a travel agency might be interested in giving away a free trip through your restaurant. Maybe a local sports team would like to team up to give away free tickets. The opportunities are endless.

Create a customer loyalty program: Send out e-newsletters to those who sign up to be in the programme, highlighting exclusive deals. Promote your loyalty program offline and online.

A Concise Guide for Operating a Restaurant

Give your menu a fresh look: If you already have a great design that works well, this may not be necessary. If you have a boring or outdated menu, however, customers may think your food is not enticing as well.

Just ask: Ask your regulars and loyal fans offline to 'Like' you on Facebook, follow you on Twitter and Pinterest, and help spread the word. Send an email, call those you have a good relationship with, and walk right up to their table while they are enjoying your restaurant.

Manage your online reputation: Review sites have become an integral part of a business's reputation, and negative reviews have the potential to harm your business. Too many negative Yelp reviews, whether true or not, will turn business away. Asking happy customers to write you a review, as well as responding personally to any negative feedback, is the best way to maintain a positive online reputation.

It may seem that I am over emphasizing on-line marketing, but this is probably the cheapest type of promotion that you can do. Still, you need an action plan to market successfully, and you can not figure out how to achieve your short-term and long-term goals unless you test the available marketing channels to gauge their effectiveness. A good breakdown for new restaurants is allocating 80 percent of your budget to digital marketing and 20 percent to traditional advertising.

Lynton Viñas

A Concise Guide for Operating a Restaurant

Remember, it matters that people "like" your restaurant Facebook pages. Yet, there must be an incentive to keep them coming to your establishment. Think out of the box. Think big, yet keep it simple. Offer lots of fun, offer deals, and offer your loyalty to the customer. This means doing your part to find out what your customers want. Use your restaurant Facebook pages for feedback, comments and to gain better understanding of your fans. Social media has changed marketing from a monologue to a dialogue. Your customers are ready to engage, converse, immerse in the brands they love; and to know that the brands they hold in high regard are relevant in their lives. Being relevant today necessitates adopting digital marketing and participating fully in social networks.

Now, I am going to make some general statements in what advertising to avoid, not because they are bad, but because in terms of bang for your money, they simply do not delivery as effectively as other forms. Newspaper advertising is very expensive, and in terms of general placements should probably be avoided. However, there are times when papers publish culinary supplements or have food sections. These sections can be effective with high end restaurants as discerning diners have a tendency to read them.

Commercial radio is a dying medium and few people listen even in their cars, as CD players are now standard in all vehicles. Additionally, different satellite streaming music stations offer commercial free music for a small monthly fee. This type of advertising is too hit and miss in today's marketplace.

The most expensive type of advertising is television, especially today where consumers have so many channels from which to choose. Unless you are a big national or regional chain, my advice is to avoid this medium because of the expense and limited reach. However, there are speciality channels that might be relative, like the Food Network, but again, the expense of advertising even on the speciality channels generally precludes the local restaurant from being able to afford commercials on them, even if there are local inserts offered. These types of channels are, again, more suited to national chains.

Do not discount any forms of advertising, but be sure to analyze its effectiveness and above all its costs. Remember what department store tycoon John Wanamaker said in 1882, "Half the money I spend on advertising is wasted. The trouble is I don't know which half." With today's technology, it is easier to find which half is wasted, and when you do it is advisable to cut that half out of your budget.

Let's take a look at some good examples of advertisements for restaurants. (See following pages.)

A Concise Guide for Operating a Restaurant

The following samples prove that sometimes simplicity and very few words can drive home the message.

A Concise Guide for Operating a Restaurant

Be very careful about what constitutes humour. The below ad might attract take-out customers, but those who live in the neighbourhood might not find it very funny.

WE DO TAKEOUT. THANK GOD.

Great Food. Bad Neighbourhood.

GEORGE'S B.B.Q

254 Dundas St. E at Sherbourne
416-648-9620

A Concise Guide for Operating a Restaurant

Lynton Viñas

A Concise Guide for Operating a Restaurant

Sometimes words are more effective than illustrations (pictures).

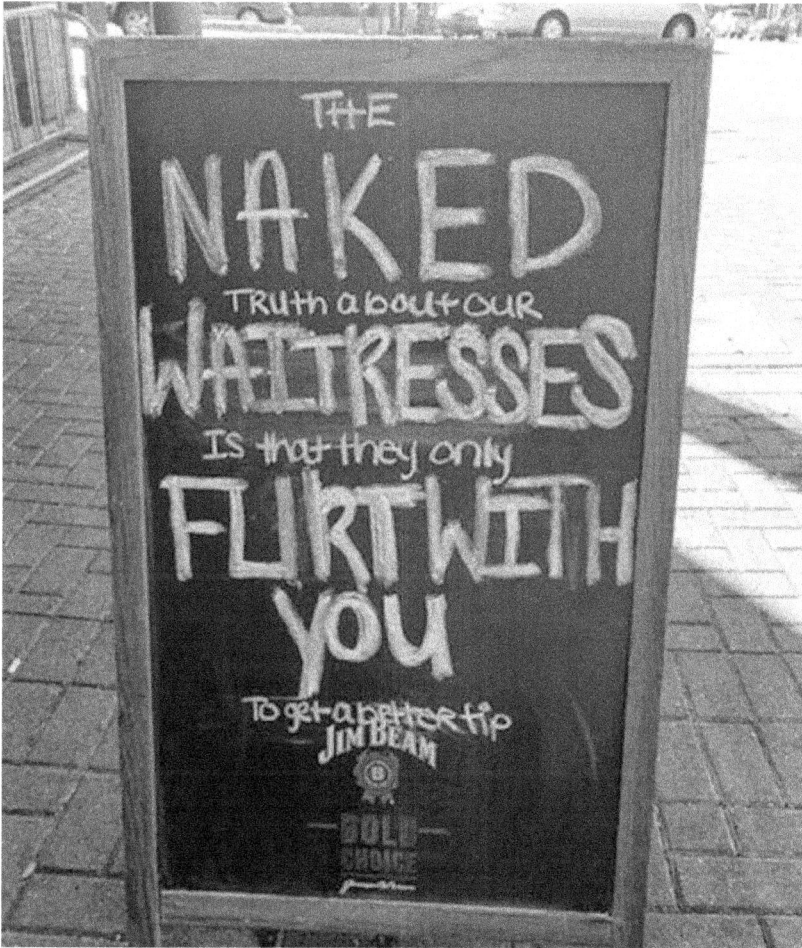

Lynton Viñas

A Concise Guide for Operating a Restaurant

Sometimes using a play on words for the restaurant name sets you apart and with just the name you have a great marketing tool. As in the name of Mother Cluckers (previous page) and Mother Tuckers on the following page, some people may be offended by the name, so be cautious. Obviously, your target market must be considered and in many cases offensive double entendres actually attract certain types of clientele.

Lynton Viñas

A Concise Guide for Operating a Restaurant

Epilogue

Knowledge

Happiness cannot be traveled to, owned, earned, worn or consumed. Happiness is the spiritual experience of living every minute with love, grace and gratitude. Never underestimate how much happiness there is in learning through experience and developing self confidence. I bring up personal experience in this guide, because I am old enough to have travelled the road of hard knocks in my life, and I am still scaling that mountain of opportunity with head unbowed, determined to reach the peak

Lynton Viñas 123

of self-confidence where the sunlight of hope basks those with determination in its warmth. If anything I said has dismayed you, I apologize, because it is not my purpose to discourage you, but rather to arm you with the most powerful weapon known to man – knowledge!

A Concise Guide for Operating a Restaurant

Do Not Miss These 3 Books by Lynton Globa Viñas

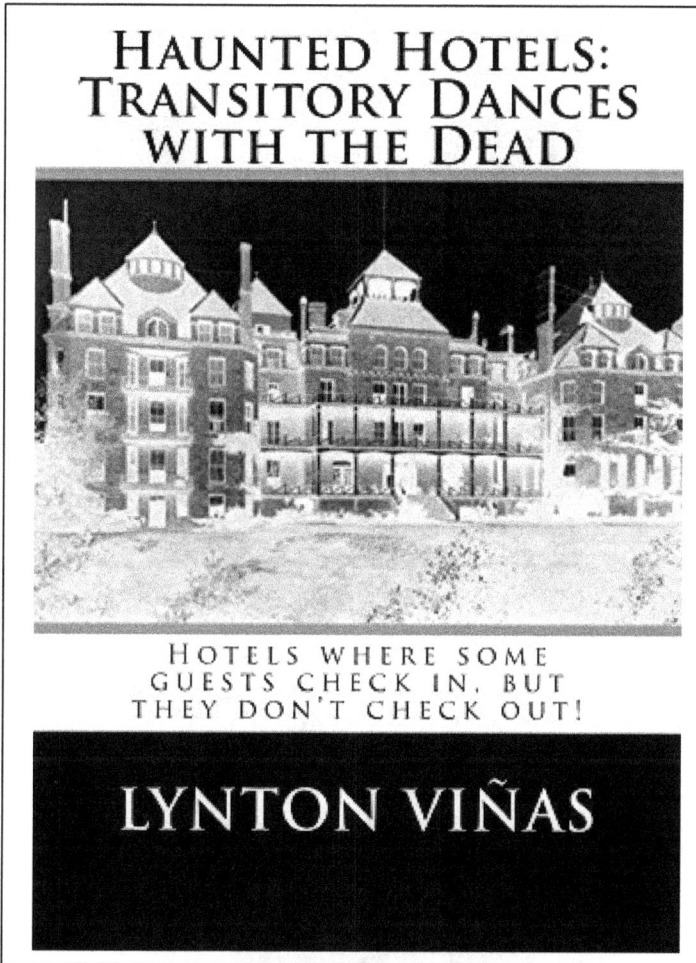

HAUNTED HOTELS:
TRANSITORY DANCES
WITH THE DEAD

HOTELS WHERE SOME
GUESTS CHECK IN, BUT
THEY DON'T CHECK OUT!

LYNTON VIÑAS

An exploration of hotels where guests have lingered after death, and occasionally decided to stroll about in discontent among current guests. Some are malevolent and some are just pranksters out for a little "after-life" fun.

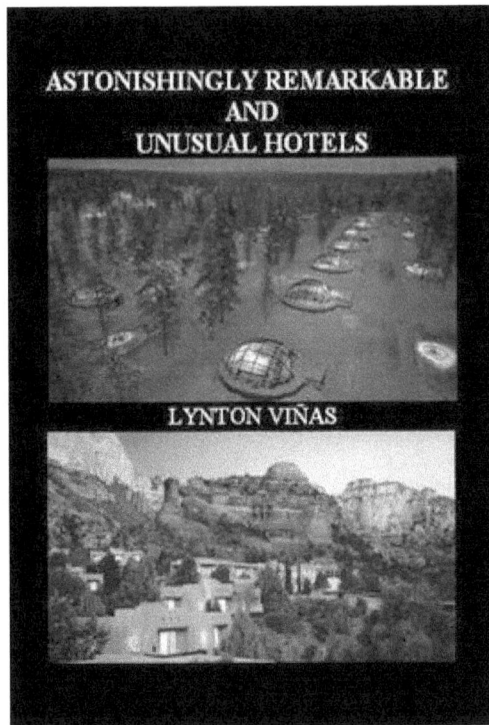

A look at the world's most unusual and iconic hotels.

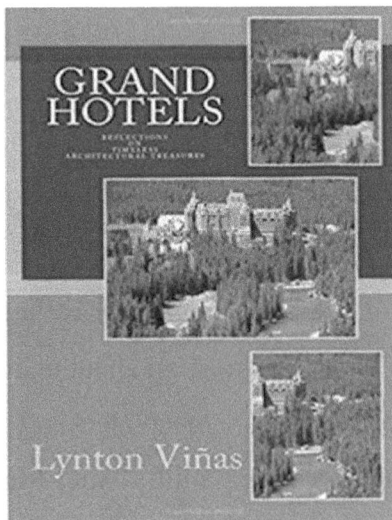

A Concise Guide for Operating a Restaurant

Bibliography (By Chapter Usage)

1.   "Marcus". Marcus. Accessed May 21, 2017.

2.   Ford, Elise Hartman (2006). Frommer's Washington, D.C. 2007, Part 3. 298. John Wiley and Sons. p. 162. ISBN 978-0-470-03849-9.

3.   Blackwell, Elizabeth Canning (2008). Frommer's Chicago 2009. 627. Frommer's. p. 123. ISBN 978-0-470-37371-2.

4.   Brown, Monique R. (January 2000). "Host your own chef's table". Black Enterprise: 122.

5.   Ford, Elise Hartman; Clark, Colleen (2006). D.C. night + day, Part 3. ASDavis Media Group. p. 25. ISBN 978-0-9766013-4-0.

6.   Miller, Laura Lea (2007). Walt Disney World & Orlando For Dummies 2008. For Dummies. p. 157. ISBN 978-0-470-13470-2.

7.   Brown, Monique R. (January 2000). "New spin on dining: Hosting a chef's table can wow guests". Black Enterprise: 122.

8.   Ellis, Steven J. R. (2004): "The Distribution of Bars at Pompeii: Archaeological, Spatial and Viewshed Analyses", Journal of Roman Archaeology, Vol. 17, pp. 371–384 (374f.)

9.   Gernet (1962:133)

10. West (1997:69–76)

11. Keifer (2002:5–7)

12. Gernet (1962:133–134)

13. Rebecca L. Spang, The Invention of the Restaurant: Paris and Modern Gastronomic Culture (Harvard University Press, 2001), ISBN 978-0-674-00685-0

14. Fierro 1996, p. 1137.

15. Metzner, Paul. Crescendo of the Virtuoso: Spectacle, Skill, and Self-Promotion in Paris during the Age of Revolution. Berkeley: University of California Press, c1998 1998. http://ark.cdlib.org/ark:/13030/ft438nb2b6/

16. Laudan, Rachel (August 2000). "Birth of the Modern Diet". Scientific American: 80–81.

17. Early Restaurants in America.

18. Eater, Bogotá (June 8, 2009). "BOGOTÁ EATS & DRINKS: Piqueteadero "El Chorote"".

19. Diccionario Comentado Del Español; Actual en Colombia. 3rd edition. by Ramiro Montoya

20. Jump up^ Leonard, Suzy Fleming (October 2, 2016). "Refining fine dining". Florida Today. Melbourne, Florida. pp. 1A, 6A, 7A. Retrieved October 12, 2017.

21. "Per Se American (New), French". Zagat. Retrieved April 29, 2017.

22. "Things to do in NYC". Fresh NYC. Retrieved August

1, 2017.

23.   "Best Modern Australian Restaurants in Melbourne". Accessed September 25, 2016.

24.   CRFA's Provincial InfoStats and Statistics Canada

25.   ReCount/NPD Group and CRFA's Foodservice Facts

26.   "Business economy – size class analysis – Statistics Explained". Epp.eurostat.ec.europa.eu. Retrieved 2013-05-02.

27.   006 U.S. Industry & Market Outlook by Barnes Reports.

28.   Phillips, Matt (16 June 2016). "No one cooks anymore". Quartz (publication). Retrieved 5 April 2017.

29.   Abrams, Rachel; Gebeloff (2017-10-31).   "Thanks to Wall St., There May Be Too Many Restaurants". New York Times. Retrieved 2017-11-01.

30.   Kerry Miller, "The Restaurant Failure Myth", Business Week, April 16, 2007. Cites an article by H.G. Parsa in Cornell Hotel & Restaurant Administration Quarterly, published August 2005.

31.   Miller, "Failure Myth", page 2 and continued on page 247.

32.   Bureau of Labor Statistics, "Occupational Employment and Wages, May 2013 35-2014 Cooks, Restaurant" online

33.   BLS, "Occupational Outlook Handbook: Food and Beverage Serving and Related Workers" (January 8, 2014) online

34.   Jiaxi Lu, "Consumer Reports: McDonald's burger ranked worst in the U.S.," [1]

35.   Nestle, Marion (1994). "Traditional Models of Healthy Eating: Alternatives to 'techno-food'". Journal of Nutrition Education. 26 (5): 241–45. doi:10.1016/s0022-3182(12)80898-3.

36.   Sibel Roller (2012). Essential Microbiology and Hygiene for Food Professionals. CRC Press. pp. ch 10.

37.   Danny May; Andy Sharpe (2004). The Only Wine Book

38.   You'll Ever Need. Adams Media. p. 221.

39.   Marketing Tips for restaurants on-line and off. Retrieved from: https://www.vision-39. 39.

40.   advertising.com/2012/08/01/restaurant-marketing-tips-success-online-and-in-the-restaurant/

www.ingramcontent.com/pod-product-compliance
Lightning Source LLC
Chambersburg PA
CBHW031729210326
41520CB00042B/1312